Performance By Design:

The Systematic Selection, Design, and Development of Performance Technologies that Produce Useful Results

Ryan Watkins

HRD Press, Inc. • Amherst • Massachusetts
ISPI • Silver Spring • Maryland

Volume III of the *Defining and Delivering Successful Professional Practice—HPT in Action* series

Series Editors:

> Roger Kaufman, Ph.D., CPT
> Dale Brethower, Ph.D.
> Richard Gerson, Ph.D., CPT

Published by:

HRD Press, Inc.
22 Amherst Road
Amherst, MA 01002
800-822-2801 (U.S. and
    Canada)
413-253-3488
413-253-3490 (fax)
www.hrdpress.com

International Society for
    Performance Improvement
1400 Spring Street
Suite 260
Silver Spring, MD 20910
301-587-8570
301-587-8573 (fax)
www.ispi.org

ISBN 10: 0-87425-949-5
ISBN 13: 978-0-87425-949-0

Production services by Jean Miller
Editorial services by Suzanne Bay
Cover design by Eileen Klockars

Table of Contents

Acknowledgments

I would like to express my appreciation and gratitude for the encouragement I have received from friends, family, and colleagues throughout the writing of this book. I would especially like to thank my family for their support: Christina Gee, Doug and Judi Watkins, and Monte and Julie Watkins.

The guidance I received from the editors of this book series, Roger Kaufman, Richard Gerson, and Dale Brethower, has added great value, and working with each of them has been a pleasure.

I am also grateful for the many colleagues and students who have participated in the development of the ideas and concepts that are found in this book, including Mike Corry, Diane Atkinson, Bill Robie, Ralph Mueller, Mary Futrell, Stephen Joel Trachtenberg, and all of the Educational Technology Leadership students at George Washington University: Doug Leigh (Pepperdine University); Ingrid Guerra (Wayne State University); Leon Sims, Robert Reiser, Walter Wager, John Keller, Marcy Driscoll, and Walter Dick (Florida State University); Scott Schaffer (Purdue University); Mike Simonson and Charlie Schlosser (Nova Southeastern University); Don Triner (U.S. Coast Guard); Lya Visser, Jan Visser, and Yusra Visser (Learning Development, Inc.); Atsusi Hirumi (University of Central Florida); and Paul Barsnica, Curtis Everett, Debbie Livingston, Stacey Lesesne, and Anthony Arnolie (National Science Foundation).

Lastly, I would like to acknowledge Bob Carkhuff and the staff at HRD Press who have contributed to the success of this book.

Ryan Watkins
June, 2006

Introduction

Improving performance is a worthy ambition for individuals and organizations alike, but the path from ambition to the accomplishment of useful results can be a difficult one to navigate. While visions, missions, and strategic plans are valuable and necessary foundations for accomplishing beneficial results, you can only improve performance by selecting, designing, and developing capable performance interventions. The Performance by Design approach and framework can systematically guide you through the processes, procedures, tools, and techniques that are most valuable in creating performance systems that achieve useful results.

The pragmatic practice of creating valuable performance improvements begins with the identification of which results are desired and how those results can be aligned with strategic objectives. This discriminating focus on the results that are to be accomplished will guide each and all of the steps that follow in systematically accomplishing performance improvements. It actually isn't until after the desired results have been defined and related to current performance within the organization that the process transitions to the assessment and selection of capable performance technologies.

A hallmark of making systematic performance improvements is postponing the selection of performance technologies until after clear objectives and evaluation criteria have been established. By delaying the decision of which solutions to implement, you can select, design, and develop a comprehensive performance improvement initiative that accomplishes desired results.

Performance by Design is an approach (or perspective) that can be used by individuals, teams, divisions, or organizations alike. It is a problem solving (and opportunity finding) approach that is focused on achieving results, and it can be applied in many situations. The accompanying Performance by Design framework then provides a systematic process for applying this performance-based approach in organizational contexts. Either in combination with other organizational development processes or as a stand-alone initiative, Performance by Design can help you accomplish desired results.

The approach and framework are offered as adaptable guides that you can—and should—customize for application within your organization, division, or unit. The processes, procedures, tools, and techniques are only of value when they are applied within organizations like yours. The precise procedures that you use to implement the approach and framework are thus less essential than your accomplishment of foundational results. Products such as prioritized definitions of which results are to be accomplished, measurable performance objectives at all levels, the assessment of potential technology interventions against performance criteria, performance technologies designed to achieve results, and implementation plans that ensure successful adoption and application are the necessary accomplishments of performance improvements that have value.

Paths to successful performance improvements are not well traveled. This book can, however, guide your way along a path that leads to the accomplishment of valuable results.

Chapter 1
What is Performance, and why do we have to design for it?

Throughout this book, our attention will center on the selection, design, and development of systems that lead directly to the accomplishment of desired and useful *performance*. While each of us can typically envision performance, more often than not we can only define it based on what we know it is not, or we simply rely on the adage *we know it when we see it*. But since performance is central in any discussion of performance improvement, we cannot afford to start out with the assumption that everyone has the same operational definition of performance.

The use, misuse, and confusion of terms in our professional language are often a significant impairment to the accomplishment of useful results.[1] The unique idioms and jargon of professional books often serve to only complicate and diminish the success of practitioners. The term *performance* has not escaped this disorientation in the literature of the past few decades.[2]

Performance, as we will discuss throughout this book, is not the same as *performing*. In designing and developing performance improvements that lead to beneficial results, a focus on performing (i.e., processes, activities, behaviors—what people do) does not ensure that valuable results will accomplished. Too often, organizations focus their attention solely on specific initiatives (e.g., quality improvement, knowledge management, information technology, mentoring, employee recruitment, balanced scorecards, and training) without first deciding which results are desired.

When we make decisions based on non-systematic processes or determine what we want to do before we define the results we want to achieve, we are focusing our attention on the *performing* rather than on the *performance*. For instance, we might buy a new car in hopes that it will result in a happier commute to the office or purchase the most up-to-date laptop thinking that it will improve our child's grades, or even follow a new diet with the intention of losing weight. Yet when we focus our attention on the activities and tools (e.g., cars, laptops, diets) rather than the desired accomplishments (e.g., happier commute, better grades, smaller waistline), rarely do we realize the results we intended or desired.

If we want to accomplish explicit and valuable results, then we must select, design, and develop the necessary support systems with a principal focus on performance. In other words, we must know which results we want to achieve.

So, what is performance? Performance is simply the useful results that we accomplish.

Hence, when designing and developing initiatives that are intended to improve performance, we must start the process with a clear and measurable definition of what results are to be accomplished. Only with comprehensive and unambiguous definitions of the results to be achieved can you make decisions about which performance technologies will accomplish those results. Separating performing from desired performance is thus essential to success; it shifts initial focus from means (i.e., performing) to ends (i.e., performance).

To illustrate this important distinction, we only have to look at a few familiar professions. For an airplane pilot, the processes of checking instruments and controlling engine speed are each elements of performing; the resulting safe landing at the airport is the desired performance. For the cleaning team in your office building, the vacuuming of floors and dusting of shelves are all tasks they perform; the clean office is the desired performance. Likewise, for the professional football player, performing is about running down the field on specific plays; individual performance can be measured by passes caught, and the assessment of team performance can be measured by the team's victories.

In all professions and for all tasks, we benefit when we can separate what it is we do (i.e., performing) from what it is that we accomplish (i.e., performance). This division allows us to focus on the performance as an objective and to subsequently select the processes for achieving that performance from all the options that are available to us.

When we accept and apply this as our definition of performance, we can now define the imperative relationship between *performing* and *performance* in all areas of our professional lives: performance is the result of performing. Specifically, performance is defined by the valuable results, accomplishments, or contributions of an individual/team or an organization, regardless of preferred or mandated processes.[3]

Performing

Brushing our teeth each night doesn't guarantee that we won't have a cavity the next time we visit the dentist, and improving the processes and tools you use for performing on the job won't necessarily result in the accomplishment of desired results. To be candid, the processes outlined in this book won't always lead to the results that you and your organization desire. There are far too many variables (time, energy, motivation, office politics, technology, personalities, incentives, and so forth)! What we do find through research and experience is that if we use results-targeted systematic processes, we can select, design, and develop many of the necessary systems for supporting performance with a high level of reliability, thus increasing the odds that the processes and resources people use to perform their jobs each day will lead to desired performance and useful results.

Desired performance is, as experience tells each of us, rarely the result of coincidence or chance. Achieving the performance that is necessary for the success of an individual, organization, or community is best ensured through use of a systematic design process. Just as for architects and engineers, accomplishing useful results requires skillful planning, quality implementation, judicious evaluation, and continual improvements. Short cuts, quick fixes, management fads, and other less-rigorous processes tend to lead to short-term changes in how people perform in the workplace, but usually do not lead to sustained improvements in performance (i.e., useful results).

Improving Performance

When an individual, team, or organization fails to consistently and efficiently accomplish the results they desire, there are many opportunities to improve performance. Managers, CEOs, supervisors, drivers, cashiers, and other individual employees routinely seek to improve performance through the actions that they take each day. Employees may come back from lunch early each day in order to meet a deadline. You may search for new ways to organize files on your computer in order to provide customers with timely answers. The truth is that most people in organizations are working to improve performance. Most of their efforts, however, are hit-or-miss activities (more or less random acts of improvement).

Although sometimes achieving valuable results, these are not the tools that organizations want to rely on to consistently achieve desired performance.

The Performance by Design approach provides practical and systematic steps for improving performance. Our approach offers several advantages over hit-or-miss improvement efforts and other organized processes that focus on performing, rather than performance.

Now let's look at five distinguishing characteristics of the Performance by Design approach.

1. It is *scalable.* The Performance by Design approach is based on a universal model for accomplishment-focused problem solving (see Figure 1.1). This foundation permits the scaling of the approach to address a range of opportunities for performance improvement. From organizational-level performance improvement initiatives (e.g., improving the overall performance in a factory that manufactures computer components) to individual performance improvement (e.g., increasing the accuracy, usefulness, and number of customer service-related calls handled by an organization's call-center operator), the Performance by Design approach can be applied with like success.

Figure 1.1: The accomplishment-focused
Six Step Problem Solving Model[4]

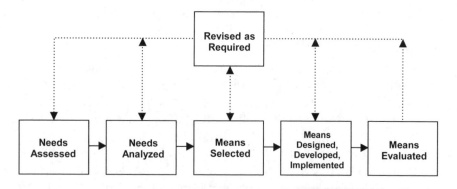

Based on the six steps of the foundational problem-solving model, you can use the approach and related framework to improve your personal performance in the workplace, guide your entire organization to the accomplishment of desired results, or lead your community by applying the same decision-making processes. The Performance by Design approach can be applied whenever there are opportunities for accomplishing useful results.

2. It is *replicable.* Individuals and organizations in most any sector of the economy can benefit from applying a performance-centered approach to their daily decision-making. The systematic processes of the Performance by Design approach and framework can be replicated throughout an organization in order to improve performance in a variety of settings, even if each setting requires distinctive results.

3. It is *systemic.* Systemic approaches to performance improvement don't rely on any specific activity, intervention, or process to accomplish desired performance. As a consequence, Performance by Design is not an instructional design approach, an electronic performance support approach, or a knowledge management approach to performance improvement. The approach and framework simply provide a systemic perspective and systematic process for accomplishing useful results at three levels: individual/team, organization, and society.

4. It is *interdisciplinary.* The Performance by Design approach incorporates processes and procedures related to strategic leadership, human resources development, systematic instructional design, communications, organizational development, industrial/organizational psychology, systems engineering, performance management, and other familiar professions. Activities related to electronic performance support, e-learning, communications, motivation, job aids, incentive systems, workplace and process redesign, organizational development, knowledge management, training, and other performance technology interventions are each recognized and included in this interdisciplinary approach to improving performance.

5. It is *performance-focused.* Lastly, and perhaps most impor-
tantly, all performance improvement efforts (including the
application of the Performance by Design approach) have
associated costs, but only a very few actually add measurable value.[5] Performance improvement activities, from the
initial identification of desired results to the evaluation of
societal outcomes, should therefore be purpose-driven and
focused on the accomplishment of useful results.

> *Performance improvement interventions always add
> cost, and only sometimes add value... The term
> "value" in "value added" and "value subtracted"
> requires that we know not only about what we "give"
> (expenses and costs), but also about what we "get
> back."*
>
> – Doug Leigh[6]

Effective performance improvement initiatives focus on the
results to be accomplished rather than the interventions that can
lead to those results. No matter if your organization is sold on the
effectiveness of leadership retreats, electronic performance support
systems, motivational seminars, process redesign, training, or balanced scorecards, the design of valuable performance systems
requires that decisions regarding which activities ought to be put
into practice be postponed until after the desired results are identified, defined, and prioritized.

Performance Worth Improving

All performance is not worth improving. In most organizations, there
are results that should be improved upon, results that should be
maintained or continued as is, and a few that should be reduced or
eliminated.[7] This diversity adds to the challenges that are already
inherent to the accomplishment of results; performance not only has
to be defined and measured, but it also has to be understood within
the context that provides for its value and worth.

Performance by Design does not begin with the assumption
that all performance is well defined and understood within every
organization. At all levels of an organization professionals too often

expend resources on performance improvement projects without a clear definition of what results are required for success. Sometimes these improvement efforts employ the latest techniques from management magazines, and other times they apply tried-and-true processes that the organization has supported in the past (without focusing on what results should be accomplished). Often these processes will even achieve results that lead individuals and organizations away from their desired goals and objectives.

Knowing what has already been accomplished and identifying the results necessary for continuing success are foundations for the effective design of performance. Achieving useful results is a multifaceted challenge. You must identify performance that should be improved upon, performance that should be maintained, and performance that has to be eliminated.

Beyond Training and Professional Development

Many organizations turn to training and related professional development activities to address numerous and varied organizational challenges (or opportunities). When the night shift slows its productivity, training is frequently the first band-aid used by managers. If a software development firm finds that the competition is increasing in market share, additional training for the company's sales team is regularly included in the next quarter's budget. For elementary schools that don't make the grade, increased requirements for professional development are time and again the dictate of superintendents and politicians who know of few other performance improvement options.

The performance problems that most organizations face today are not, however, the result of a lack of skill or knowledge (the focus of most training and educational activities). In fact, research suggests that less than 20% of performance problems can be resolved with a training solution.[8] All solutions, even those solutions that that we are most familiar with and comfortable implementing, should be considered within a larger performance context. Well-designed training can, for example, have a significant impact on performance—especially when it is accompanied by other necessary performance improvement activities that are aligned with the desired accomplishments. Likewise, when performance problems are not the result of a deficiency in skill and/or knowledge, training, and other professional development activities alone are not going to result in enduring performance improvements.

Training and education activities are intended to develop skills and/or increase knowledge. When they are well done, they result in learning, and learning is typically a necessary (but not sufficient) prerequisite for performance. Without action, learning by itself will not lead to desired performance, so the connections are critical in determining the appropriate relationships of training with other performance-improvement interventions. Performance problems and opportunities to improve within organizations, after all, come in a thousand varieties; you must combine performance technologies on a project-by-project basis.

The Performance Pyramid (see Figure 1.2) provides a useful framework for defining the relationships between performance solutions. It illustrates the foundational supports that must be in place to sustain performance, and shows their relationship with other performance interventions.

Consistent with an emphasis on systemic performance improvement, this framework rests on the premise that significant accomplishments result when the underpinnings that support performance are in place. At the foundation, the vision, mission, and objectives represent the common direction and goals of any group. It is particularly useful to consider this foundation in three dimensions: societal, organizational, and individual/team (which aligns performance improvement efforts with the three levels of results found in the Organizational Elements Model[9]).

As a consequence, the solutions used to improve performance must be based on these three foundational elements if they are to have the necessary support for success. The foundation in many ways represents the culture of an organization. Unfortunately, it is common for an organization to lack a clear sense of direction, even after decades of annual management retreats. (Witness the number of dusty binders labeled "strategic plan" on a manager's bookshelf.) This condition is the antithesis of what is found in high-performing organizations.

Figure 1.2. Performance Pyramid with Integrated Strategic Planning[10]

The pyramid format also illustrates the supporting relationships of six building blocks for performance: expectations and feedback; tools, environment, processes; rewards, recognition, and incentives; motivation and self-concept; performance capacity; and competence. Accomplishments suffer when these foundations do not support desired performance—that is, if one or more of the blocks are missing or if the blocks are not aligned with one another.

For example, if insurance adjusters are trained to process claims in a manner that is not consistent with the computer systems available to do the job, there will be an alignment problem, and the same is true if "solitary" performance technologies are introduced in an organization. Misalignment can also be produced if the technology tools are provided to the workforce but the rewards, recognition, or incentive systems do not support the use of technology; or if employees are recruited without the necessary background knowledge and skills to perform the basic tasks required by the job. Alignment troubles like these are common factors leading to performance problems.

The building blocks of the Pyramid are interdependent. Although the strength and direction of the relationships between the blocks has still not been formally examined through research, the components of the pyramid provide a valuable framework for codifying and organizing the relationship between various performance technologies and acts as a reminder of the multiple factors to consider when debating what to do to improve performance.

Performance Technologies

Technologies represent in our society the newest and most valuable ideas and creations that leaders in any profession have to offer. Whether it is the latest in computer components or the most recent procedures for relieving the pain associated with heart surgery, technologies embody what a profession has learned from its past, while offering a glimpse of what may be possible in the future. Performance technologies are no different. Performance technology builds on the strengths of many closely associated fields of study and practice (e.g., business management, human resources, instructional design, educational technology, information technology, strategic planning, systems analysis and design, human factors engineering, interpersonal and mass communications, industrial/organizational psychology), and has developed into a discipline with its own theories, models, scholars, and practitioners.

Technology is often used to refer to computers, electronic devices, gadgets, and other tools made of silicon chips, magnets, and other mechanisms. These are, however, just one set of tools for achieving useful results. The term must take on a much broader definition for those who are not interested in selling a product or preconceived solution. Improving human and organizational performance requires that we view *technology* simply as the identification and resolution of problems.[11] Thus, performance technologies are a wide-range of solutions and activities that we can use to achieve results.

Many of today's performance technologies are applications of information technologies (e.g., DVD-based training, video-conference mentoring, motivational books in MP3 file formats), but you should not rely solely on hardware or software to improve the performance of individuals and organizations. The development of a mentoring program for new employees, for example, does not necessarily require any investments in information technology (i.e., computers, networks, software applications). The same is true for changes to recognition systems, development of new organizational policies, systematic instructional design, and/or workflow redesign efforts. Each of these can be effective performance technologies with or without the addition of information technologies. Assess the capacity of a performance technology to accomplish desired results and if appropriate use it in combination with other performance improvement efforts as a set of solutions.

Effective approaches to performance technology do not begin with any specific performance improvement solution in mind (i.e., a solution in search of a problem). Rather, by drawing on the diverse solutions provided through the research and experience in closely related professions, the performance technologist increases the ability to align one or more performance improvement activities with the results that must be accomplished. These performance technology solutions can include motivational signs, work-flow redesign, changes in accounting models, training on new software applications, customer service workshops, online job-aids, new information technology networking infrastructure, revised employee selection criteria, or some fusion of the thousands of other activities that have the potential to improve individual and organizational performance. This diversity of tools and techniques for accomplishing useful results is what differentiates performance technology from each of the disciplines that it draws upon.

Throughout this book, we will explain how performance technologies can be used as specific interventions or sets of solutions to achieve performance objectives. Keep in mind that most performance improvement efforts are not successful if they employ only a single performance technology (or solution). A comprehensive performance improvement initiative includes the systemic application of multiple performance technologies. Hence, accomplishments are typically facilitated by sets of solutions that are comprised of integrated performance technologies (see Figure 1.3).

Figure 1.3. Systemic performance improvement initiatives

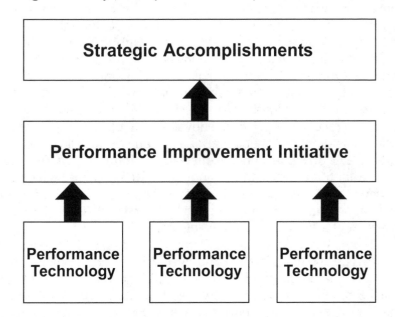

Designing the "right" blend of activities is at the heart of performance improvement. The "right" blend for one organization may not, however, be the "right" blend for another organization. Similarly, the activities that will improve performance in one division of an organization might also differ from the activities that will be successful in other divisions of the same organization. Improvement initiatives must therefore not be based on preconceived notions about any technology (e.g., e-learning, leadership seminars, recruitment tactics, empowerment retreats).

Nonetheless, most of us will begin each new effort to improve performance with a solution in mind. It's comfortable, but not advisable. Professionals typically have more experience with some technology solutions than with others (e.g., motivation support, instructor-led training, information technologies vs. process redesign, incentive systems, mentoring). As a result, we are more likely to draw upon our experience again and again when making recommendations. This seems like an appropriate approach, particularly if they have produced results in the past.

Unfortunately, too often our perspectives of available perform-ance technologies are defined by past experiences, glossy market-ing brochures, or half-hour conference presentations. Try not to begin the performance improvement process with an "out of the box" or "one size fits all" solution, since this will impede or stymie your success. Training departments, for instance, tend to think that most performance problems are best resolved through training solutions (whether or not the performance issues are linked to defi-cits in knowledge and skills). External consultants who specialize in motivation seminars or rewards systems will likewise link most per-formance problems with insufficient support in these areas. Usually these are not unethical practices, but it is better to counteract any preconceived notions about which solutions will best improve per-formance. Use a systematic, results-focused approach to ensure that a variety of alternative performance technologies are consid-ered, compared, and evaluated.

If you want to improve performance, it is best to compare a variety of practical technologies that are capable of accomplishing valuable results. It is then through the systematic processes of assessing, analyzing, selecting, designing, developing, implement-ing, evaluating, and improving that significant improvements in performance are achieved.

Novice and Expert Applications

The employees of most organizations come to work each day with a diverse range of skills, knowledge, attitudes, experiences, and ambitions. Performance improvement efforts are then most effective when they offer a systematic process that can be replicated, cus-tomized, and scaled to meet the unique requirements of most any organization. The Performance by Design approach uses a variety of step-by-step guides, heuristics, and job aids to help individuals or groups in most any organization improve upon the results that are currently being achieved. The approach and framework neverthe-less are not intended to be rigid.

Experts in many professions develop valuable problem-solving skills by building, merging, challenging, and making routine the step-by-step processes that were most helpful to them as novices. From mathematics and biology to psychology and music, profes-sionals typically begin their careers by carefully applying the par-ticular methods and processes of their field of expertise. Often reluctant to modify those processes as novices, they generally experiment, vary, challenge, or internalize many of the procedures that once required reference guides for success. As their experience and confidence grows, they will apply these skills instinctively when solving increasingly complex problems.

The step-by step guides included in this book suggest a broad approach for improving performance. For those who are new to performance improvement, these are introductory tools and methods that should be applied in the recommended sequence. As you gain experience, skills, and knowledge, these algorithms will slowly emerge as everyday practice. They can then be matched or altered to your expertise and experiences, rather than adopted as a sequential process. (Although your approach should remain systemic and your processes systematic.)

Most approaches to improving performance are initially presented as step-by-step guides that can be applied in a variety of contexts. Novice technologists will predictably apply these approaches carefully and systematically, while experts will often interlace the steps with other tools, techniques, models, and processes. The applied value of an approach or framework for improving performance is thus defined by its flexibility, providing useful tools for novices and experts alike.

The Performance by Design Framework

Frameworks provide flexible, scalable, and systematic processes for improving individual and/or organizational performance. The Six-Step Problem Solving model (from Figure 1.1), for instance, offers an adaptable process you can use to resolve formidable challenges. As a general model, this six-step process offers a foundational guide that you can either apply methodically or customize based on your professional experience.

Whether you are resolving problems or capitalizing on opportunities, you can then supplement the general problem-solving process with the more detailed steps of the Performance by Design framework. Specifically, the systematic steps of the framework focus your efforts on the selection, design, and development of performance technologies in relation to the third and forth steps of the problem-solving process (see Figure 1.4). (Previous and subsequent steps of the problem solving model are then addressed in greater detail by accompanying books of this series.)

Figure 1.4. The Integration of Performance by Design
in the Six-Step Problem Solving Process

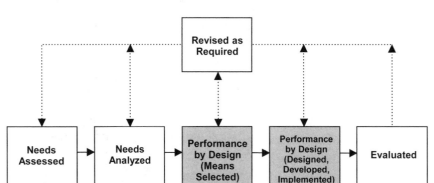

The Performance by Design framework defines seven primary steps that should be aligned, integrated, and completed in order to accomplish useful results at societal (mega), organizational (macro), and individual/team (micro) levels. Although the steps are illustrated in a sequence from top to bottom (see Figure 1.5), in application they are actually quite fluid. As you build expertise in applying the framework, you will typically begin to create your own performance improvement process. The role of the framework in guiding professional practice is thereby extensively shaped by your experience and the context in which you are applying the related steps, without sacrificing the systemic perspective or the systematic processes. (Each step in the Performance by Design framework will be described sequentially in the remaining chapters of this book.)

Figure 1.5. The Performance by Design framework

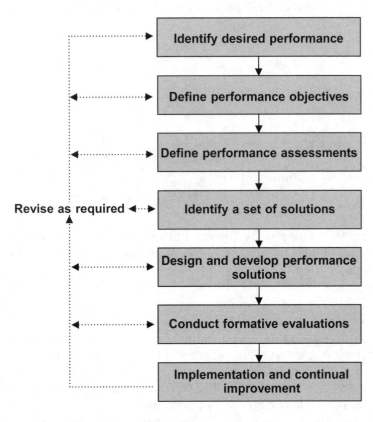

An approach, framework, or model can't, however, actually accomplish desired performance improvements. It can only offer guidance to skilled professionals who will define success, consider multiple performance technologies, design an appropriate set of solutions, develop performance technologies, and continuously improve their efforts. The processes, procedures, tools, and techniques in this book can guide your improvement efforts, but you will have to apply these resources for useful results to be accomplished.

"Case in Point"

Throughout the book, we have included many examples and illustrations for the concepts, processes, and products described in the improvement process. However, these examples often describe the application of single step as it applies to discrete industries or business sectors, so the "big picture" of how you can use the approach to improve performance may be lost without a running example. In response, we will use a case study to illustrate how the individual steps within the framework can be integrated and applied collectively. The "Case In Point" example focuses on a single fictional organization, Pill Containers Inc., with similarities to most organizations.

Case in Point

The fictional organization we are calling Pill Containers, Inc. is a decade-old business that specializes in the production of pharmaceutical containers used by community drug stores throughout the United States. With more than 500 employees, Pill Containers is structured in functional units (manufacturing, sales, design, accounting, and other divisions). Two manufacturing facilities are in operation. The second facility opened 18 months ago in a neighboring community. Pill Containers averages more than 2.5 million dollars in sales each year, but has several opportunities for growth on the horizon if the company's leaders can resolve a handful of internal performance problems and capitalize on a number of performance opportunities.

Two years ago, Steve Landon was hired as a performance improvement manager within the human resources division of the organization. Having worked for several organizations that were experiencing similar growing pains, Landon knew that a results-focused performance improvement initiative that spans across all divisions of the organization would be a necessary ingredient in preparing Pill Containers for desired growth.

We will follow the life-cycle of this performance improvement effort from beginning to end to supplement the other examples scattered throughout the book. Use the Pill Containers case study to reflect on how you can apply the various steps in the Performance by Design approach and framework in your organization to accomplish useful results.

Chapter Summary

The Performance by Design approach and framework focus performance improvement efforts on the accomplishment of useful results. By differentiating the desired results to be achieved (i.e., performance) from the processes, tools, and resources used by individuals and organizations (i.e., performing), the approach provides a scalable, replicable, systemic, interdisciplinary model for improving the performance. The steps as illustrated in the framework seem rigid, but in application they are actually fluid and dynamic. This allows you to apply the framework in a variety of contexts by integrating the approach with other performance improvement resources and experiences.

Each step in the Performance by Design framework will be described sequentially in the following chapters.

Chapter 1 Notes

1. A glossary of terms is found at the end of the book.

2. Watkins and Leigh, 2001

3. Watkins and Wedman, 2003

4. Kaufman, Oakley-Brown, Watkins and Leigh, 2003

5. Leigh, 2003; Brethower and Smalley, 1998

6. Leigh, 2003

7. Leigh, 2003; Leigh, 2006

8. Stolovich, 2000; Clark and Estes, 2002

9. Kaufman, 2006; Kaufman, Kaufman, Oakley-Brown, Watkins and Leigh, 2003; Watkins and Leigh, 2001

10. Watkins and Wedman, 2003; based on Wedman and Graham, 1998, and Wedman and Diggs, 2001; also see Gilbert, 1978

11. See Gerson, 2006

Section One:
Defining Performance

The design of performance systems begins with a focus on defining the results (i.e., performance) that will guide subsequent decisions. From analyzing the strategic plans and aligning performance objectives to defining results criteria and selecting appropriate performance assessments, Section One presents tools, techniques, processes, and procedures for ensuring that all performance improvement initiatives accomplish useful results.

We will begin by identifying performance expectations in terms of useful results to be accomplished at the societal, organizational, and individual/team levels as the essential first step in improving performance. These goals and objectives will subsequently guide all of our decisions and lead to valuable performance improvements.

Figure 2.0. The Performance by Design framework

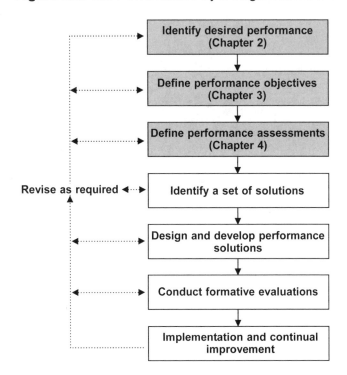

Chapter 2
Identify Desired Performance

Introduction

To improve performance we must first describe the desired performance (i.e., results) that will guide our selection, design, and development of performance technologies. The desired performance of an organization, division, project team, or even an individual are characteristically very challenging to identify, define, and measure without a systematic process to focus your efforts. Goals such as "working to be number one," "on the cutting edge," or "one step ahead of the competition" can provide motivation, but they do not offer clear and measurable objectives by which important decisions can be made, measured, and evaluated.

Most of us like to define our "success" by our accomplishments (e.g., "I graduated from college with a 4.0 GPA" or "I climbed Mt. Everest"). It's not, however, always easy to determine which accomplishments we will use to define success when improving performance. For starters, our view of "success" represents only one perspective on what results should be achieved. (A point of view that is routinely different from the perspectives of others inside and outside of our organizations.) "Success" to you might, for example, be reducing the time that customers are on the phone with technical support staff, but "success" to clients might be getting accurate information from the support staff.

Similarly, you might consider a new learning management system to be successful when a targeted number of employers use the system. However, supervisors might prefer a definition of "success" based on the results that employees contribute to the organization after completing their training.

Your definitions of success provide the criteria by which you will assess your accomplishments. If achievements are evaluated without clear and agreed upon criteria, mistakes will be made that distract from performance improvements.

To avoid making such mistakes:

1. Don't define success in vague terms.

2. Don't assume that you know which results define success for everybody.

3. Don't define success only from one perspective.

4. Don't wait to define success. Define it before any solutions are selected.

5. Don't define success in terms of processes or activities. Define it in terms of results and accomplishments.

Nevertheless, most of us base our decisions on some definition of "success," even when our informal definitions are limited or flawed. Informal definitions (i.e., those not derived through a systematic process) can shift the focus of a performance improvement project away from the achievement of valuable results. Further, initiatives that proceed without a clear and agreed upon definition as to which results constitute "success" can suffer from a lack a direction and fail to achieve any results. Use the diverse perspectives that partners (internal and external to your organization) bring to any project to develop meaningful performance requirements and an unambiguous definition of success.

When specifying the desired performance that will guide the selection, design, and development of an effective performance improvement effort, start with a review of the strategic plans for your organization and its partners. Then assess the needs and analyze the context to put the strategic ambitions (and intentions) in perspective. Together, information and data from each of these processes will provide the performance objectives that you later use to guide decisions. Figure 2.1 illustrates the relationship of these three processes in defining strategic direction.

Figure 2.1. Processes for defining strategic direction

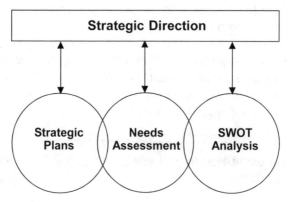

In this chapter, we will focus on defining the performance indicators of success. From the strategic plans of your organization and its partners, you will identify the goals and objectives that guide decision making. In addition, you will expand your definition of success by examining performance discrepancies and the contextual drivers for strategic direction-setting by using the results of needs assessment and SWOT analysis efforts (see Figure 2.2). Based on these processes, you can align your performance improvement efforts with the strategic objectives of the internal and external organizational partners.

Figure 2.2. Process to identify desired performance

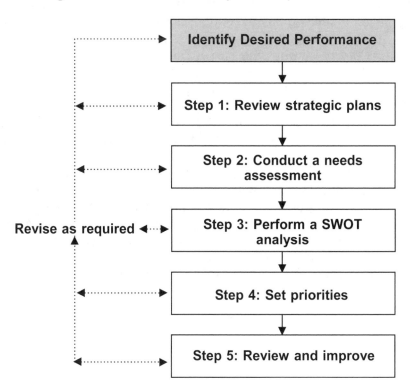

Strategic Planning and Alignment

The improvement of performance and the accomplishment of useful results begin with a review of the strategic goals and objectives of everyone involved in the performance system: your organization, direct clients who purchase your products or services, clients of your clients, the suppliers who provide resources to your organization, as well as contributing or impacted community groups. Each of these partners in the performance system is critical to the success of the others (including your performance improvement efforts). Only when working together can any of the mutually supporting groups accomplish the useful results they desire. The goals and objectives of the partner organizations are therefore an ideal starting place for defining desired performance.

The strategic goals and objectives of your organization and its partners are not always the same. Given your unique businesses, each will likely have some distinctive goals and ambitions. Nevertheless, there will also be many goals and objectives that are shared among the organizational partners. The combination of unique and shared ambitions provides important information for defining what results are expected from any performance improvement effort.

Most organizations strive for future-oriented strategic goals. Proactive plans can't be defined when an organization is only looking internally for guidance. Future opportunities (and obstacles) are by and large found outside of the organization through input from clients, clients' clients, and other partners in the community (see Figure 2.3). Reactive or conventional plans begin and end within the organization. To accomplish useful results, you will want to focus on those strategic intentions that are future-focused.

Figure 2.3. Future-oriented or proactive planning vs. conventional or reactive planning orientations[1]

Conventional Planning and Assessment (Reactive)

Organizational methods, resources, culture, structure, and results		Current societal results

Future-Oriented Planning and Assessment (Proactive)

Organizational methods, resources, culture, structure, and results		Desired societal results

Step One: Review strategic plans.

Desired results: An inventory of strategic goals and objectives for the organization and its partners.

Performance improvement efforts ideally add value for partners internal and external to your organization. Equally, these partners will be critical in determining which results define your success. Begin by first identifying the results that your internal and external partners are looking for: direct results that are achieved by performance technologies (e.g., more quality parts per thousand, improved safety of shipping operations), as well as indirect results that are accomplished by performance systems (e.g., long-term client satisfaction, product safety, reduced production costs). These desired results will shape your decision making as well as define how you and your partners later evaluate success. It is important to both identify and align the strategic directions (i.e., goals and objectives) of all organizational partners.

Request strategic plans, annual reports, and other direction-setting documents from your organization's internal and external partners. These documents will identify both the long-term and short-term objectives of the organizations; which will in turn help you determine their organizational priorities, objectives, and resources.

As you review these documents, focus on the performance that each organization is committed to accomplishing. These are sometimes defined in a vision statement or mission objective, but are more often described in detail in the long-term and short-term objectives of specific units within the organization. As you review the strategic plans, inventory the specific results that are guiding each organization's decisions (see Table 2.1).

Table 2.1. Relating performance objectives with
current organizational processes

Goal or Objective	Organization	Source
Reduce production costs by 25% over the next three years	Light Switches, Inc. (supplier)	2007 annual report
Expand product line to include three environment-friendly alternative lighting options	Local Office Supplies (client)	2008 strategic plan

For example, let's say your organization is in the business of producing desk lamps and your specific performance improvement initiative is focused on reducing the number of lamps that are shipped without a working switch. To begin, you should examine the strategic documents of those organizations that supply you with cords, switches, and other components necessary for a working lamp. In reviewing their strategic plans, identify performance objectives that define what results they intend to accomplish in the future. Also look for goals related to significant projects they are implementing for improving the quality and safety of their products (e.g., no injuries or deaths from electrical shocks).

Internal partners within your organization may also provide valuable information for defining the criteria of successful performance improvements. Your measures of success might change dramatically if you learn from the marketing department, for instance, that there is a new sales promotion for your product line of desk lamps that features a quality guarantee upon delivery. Similarly, the manager of the manufacturing facility may add a perspective on desired performance that has more to do with the production capacity of the workers than the number of lamps that get returned. All of which is important for you to know before making any decisions about what performance technologies should be used within your organization to improve performance.

Also, identify the performance expectations of your direct clients; any performance improvements you make should contribute to their success as well. If you provide lamps to an office supply store, information on the store's sales objectives for your products (as compared to the products of your competitors), percentage of returned products, and/or their objectives for expanding their business over the next five years are all important.

Lastly, the indirect clients of your organization (i.e., your clients' clients and other partners in the community) represent another important partner in any project. Identifying and defining their expectations is an essential ingredient to success. Inquire about how consumers use your lamps to accomplish their goals, what performance expectations they have of your organization, what considerations are necessary to ensure the safe use of your lamps, and/or what results they would measure to define the success of a performance improvement initiative. Society is the ultimate client of all that an organization uses, does, produces, and delivers, and it should be included as a partner in all performance improvement efforts.

If the organization's partners do not have documents that you can use to identify or verify the strategic objectives of their organization, you should meet with the partners to discuss the desired results they intend to achieve (independent of your performance improvement initiative, as well as through your efforts). Most will give you detailed descriptions of their long- and short-term objectives when asked. Be alert, however, for vague statements that are not linked to measurable results. These "fuzzy" objectives might be of some value in providing general direction, but you really want the specific results they expect to achieve in the near and distant future.

Case in Point

The executive leaders at Pill Containers go on a strategic planning retreat twice a year at the local country club. The organization, however, has only a few documents that guide their long-term decisions. In addition, the organization's vision and mission seem to shift from year to year. Organizational leaders have done an excellent job growing the company in the past, but there is no clearly stated direction for the future. Realizing this, Landon and his team knew that they would have to find documents to supplement the formal strategic plans of the organization.

Members of the performance improvement team collected information from internal and external sources that might be helpful in defining a strategic direction for the company. The team collected annual reports from direct clients that described their recent acquisitions and future goals. Indirect clients provided information regarding the future of automated prescription machines, growth in the pharmaceutical industry, and alternatives to pills that are being created as substitute delivery systems for medicines. The team reviewed surveys and other data from across the country and identified many consumer trends related to the distribution and consumption of prescription medications.

Not wanting to stop there, the team also interviewed suppliers to identify their strategic goals. When one supplier suggested that new technologies in developing plastics offer new opportunities, the performance improvement team started to see how Pill Containers could change over the next decade. Little of this information would have been news to the organizational leaders, but this was the first time that anyone documented input regarding the strategic direction for immediate use in daily decision making.

By itself, a list of goals and objectives can't guide the selection, design, and development of useful performance technologies. The unique and shared intentions of the organizational partners must now be connected. Use the Organizational Elements Model (OEM) to categorize the intentions of each organizational partner. The organizational elements describe and relate what an organization uses, does, produces, delivers, and contributes (see Figure 2.4).[2] By categorizing the goals and objectives of each organization, you can identify synergies, discrepancies, and redundancies, as well as many other opportunities to improve performance.

Figure 2.4. The Organizational Elements Model
■

Societal outcomes (i.e., Mega-level results)

↕

Organizational outputs (i.e., Macro-level results)

↕

Individual/Team products (i.e., Micro-level results)

↕

Processes (i.e., activities, behaviors)

↕

Inputs (i.e., resources, technologies)

Goals and objectives that are focused on the accomplishment of community and societal outcomes (i.e., mega-level results) should be classified as "strategic." These define the contributions to be delivered to external clients and how those accomplishments will be measured. Strategic goals and objectives provide the best starting place for improving performance, since they are shared among all of the organizational partners.

Objectives at the societal level are not defined by a single organization, nor is it expected that any one organization will accomplish them on their own. Strategic objectives are the shared ambitions of the individuals, organizations, groups, and other partners that represent our shared communities and society (e.g., no loss of life nor elimination or reduction of levels of survival, self-sufficiency, or quality of life from substance abuse, disease, discrimination, etc.)[3]. To define their mission, organizations can then identify from these strategic intentions (which inherently aligns organizational outputs with societal outcomes).

Do not worry, however, if your review of strategic plans doesn't identify any "strategic" goals or objectives. Simply make a note of this and later on you can consider systemic strategic planning as an optional performance technology for helping your organization define the results it wants to contribute, along with its partners, to the shared community and society.

Likewise, categorize intentions that are focused on the accomplishment of organizational outputs (i.e., macro-level results) as "tactical" plans, and intentions that are focused on the accomplishment of individual/team products (i.e., micro-level results) as "operational" plans. Most likely your organization and its partners will each have ample goals at the tactical and operational level. Nevertheless, if your review of strategic planning documents doesn't identify consistent goals or objectives at these levels, then systemic strategic planning is again probably a performance technology solution you will want to consider later on.

Together, goals and objectives from each classification (i.e., strategic, tactical, and operational) constitute an integrated and systemic set of long-term intentions (see Table 2.2).[4] Aligned objectives at each level are valuable guides for making decisions, while gaps, redundancies, or misalignments of objectives are typically opportunities for performance improvements. Use the objectives identified at each level as the starting place for your performance-focused needs assessment.

Table 2.2. Three Levels of Focus and Planning[5]

Level of Results	Level of Planning and Focus	Examples
Societal outcomes (Mega-level)	*Strategic*: Results to be contributed to external partners, clients' clients, and the shared society	• Profits over time (not just one-shot) • Self-sufficient citizens • Zero disabilities from accidents • Zero starvation
Organizational outputs (Macro-level)	*Tactical:* Results to be delivered by the organization to external clients	• Delivered vehicle • Discharged patient • Competent graduate • Dividends • Non-polluting exhaust
Individual/team products (Micro-level)	*Operational:* Results to be produced by individuals or teams for internal partners and clients	• Delivered technical advice • DVD training materials • Manual for executive coaches • Component of automobile brake system

Assessing Needs

In practical terms, assessment is a process used by individuals or organizations to determine the value or worth of something.[6] Assessments often relate to the determination of monetary values, but professionals who focus on improving results pragmatically focus on the assessment of performance. Value or worth is then derived from the relationship of current performance (i.e., results being achieved) and desired performance (i.e., results required for continuing success). This process is commonly referred to as "needs assessment," although not all needs assessments focus on performance and results.[7]

When reviewing strategic plans and direction-setting documents for your organization and its partners, you should categorize results into three levels: societal (i.e., mega level), organizational (i.e., macro level), and individual/team (i.e., micro level). These levels of performance also define three levels of needs assessment (see Figure 2.4). For each level where you have objectives that define desired results (i.e., What Should Be) and data regarding current results (i.e., What Is), you should complete a needs assessment. Ideally you will complete needs assessments at all three levels.[8]

Figure 2.4. Needs Assessments at Three Levels of Results[9]

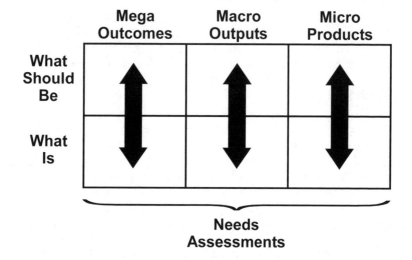

Assessments at all three levels help us to determine or approximate the value of various discrepancies identified between current and desired results. This assessment (or valuation) of results provides an essential ingredient in the identification and prioritization of the desired performance. Only when you have defined both the current performance and desired performance in measurable terms can you make an assessment of their relative value to individuals or teams, the organization, and/or the community of external partners. Value is then measured by the comparison of estimated costs (monetary and non-monetary costs, such as political costs) for closing gaps between current and desired performance, and the associated costs for not closing the gaps at each level.[10]

Performance-focused assessments define "needs" as the discrepancies between current results and the results required for the accomplishment of objectives (see Figure 2.5).[11] These results-based needs are then best assessed by an assortment of measures. For example, the quality of client services might be important to your organization and its partners. If so, don't rely on a single measure (such as client satisfaction surveys) to accurately measure the need between current and/or desired results. You would be better served with an expanded set of measures (e.g., filed complaints, interviews with customer service representatives, surveys of sales staff, focus groups with clients, organizational performance records, repurchase rates, referral rates, and/or the number of contracts that were extended upon the completion of initial work). These various measures, each discrete factors of quality, can provide you with a more accurate picture of the quality of client service and the current need.

Figure 2.5. Relating needs to discrepancies between What Is and What Should Be

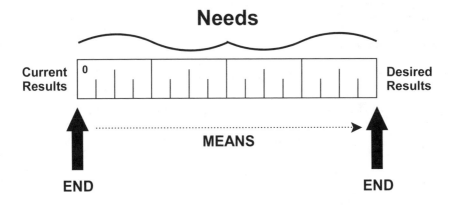

Combine both "hard" and "soft" data, as well as qualitative and quantitative data, to define gaps between the current and desired accomplishments (see Table 2.4). This will broaden your perspective and define multiple measures for each need. Hard data refers to the results of those measures that are externally verifiable; soft data are the results of those measures that cannot be externally verified.

Table 2.3. Examples of data-collection tools and
techniques for each data type

	Hard (externally verifiable data)	**Soft** (not externally verifiable data)
Quantitative (numeric expressions of a variable)	• Performance data • Budget analysis	• Likert-type scale surveys[12] • Performance ratings
Qualitative (non-numeric expressions of a variable)	• Focus groups • Analysis of a list- serve • Document review • Multi-source performance observations	• Opinion surveys • Individual interviews • Single-source performance observations

The types of data you collect in supporting a needs assessment
should be closely related to the levels of results being assessed. In
completing a needs assessment, use the organizational goals and
objectives to define what results should be accomplished at the
societal, organizational, and individual/team levels.

Step Two: Conduct a needs assessment.

*Desired results: A record of discrepancies between desired and
current performance.*

To begin a needs assessment, you will again want to draw on the
documents that establish the strategic direction for your organization and its partners. (This is why we started with a review of strategic plans.) The results and accomplishments defined in those
documents will provide the first identification of desired (i.e., What
Should Be) results for the needs assessment.

If your organization (and its partners) are like most, the majority
of objectives from your review of strategic direction-setting documents are at the organizational and individual/team levels. In
response, you will want to work with internal and external partners

to define the related societal objectives that should be accomplished; then review the organizational and individual/team objectives in order to verify their alignment with the identified societal contributions. This can either be done as part of the needs assessment or offered as a potential performance technology (i.e., systemic strategic planning) during the selection of performance solutions.

When you have identified goals or objectives for each level, determine appropriate measures for each (if performance indicators are not included in the objective). For example, if a team objective is to produce a useful customer service survey, then you will identify measures of how survey usefulness can be assessed. These measures then define the data that must be collected in order to assess both current and desired levels of performance. For instance, if an objective for your organization is the delivery of safe football helmets, use measures of production, delivery, customer acceptance, player injuries, and other factors as measures for both current (i.e., What Is) and desired (i.e., What Should Be) performance.

You should identify two or three associated performance measures for each performance objective. This ensures that you are capturing an accurate picture of any gaps between current and desired performance (i.e., needs). As these measures for each performance objective are defined, come up with a process for collecting the necessary data and apply it systematically with your organizational partners. Ideally, you will collect both hard and soft data for each objective, using qualitative and quantitative data collection techniques.

Don't rely on the assumptions that desired results are known, agreed upon, and similarly evaluated throughout the organization (and among the organization's partners). This can be dangerous. However, when you collect data on both current and desired results, your needs assessment won't reflect (and rely on) an assumption that desired performance has already been well defined and measured. You will instead be able to identify gaps or discrepancies using a consistent scale of measurement and be able to see real and/or perceived differences between current individual, organizational, and societal performance and the desired or required performance.

After you identify and collect data regarding desired and current performance at each level, calculate the discrepancies between current and desired results (i.e., desired results minus current results). Then classify these discrepancies as either needs or strengths. When current results are not meeting the necessary requirements of the desired results, you have identified a need. Similarly, when current results meet or exceed desired expectations, you have identified a strength on which the organization can capitalize.

Collecting this kind of data allows you to prioritize discrepancies by examining the location of the gaps along the uniform scale. For example, while the gaps for two distinct data elements may have similar values (e.g., 2 points along the Likert-type scale), their perceived importance may vary greatly, depending on location of the gaps (e.g., desired performance of 5 vs. desired performance of 3).

For qualitative data, which is not numeric, you should identify themes or trends that can be compared. Use a content analysis to summarize findings from open-ended survey questions, interviews, focus groups, observations, and other qualitative techniques. Common themes and trends can then be identified. To provide a context for each theme or trend, find examples (such as quotes from participants) to support each finding. You can then make systematic comparisons of the data.

By collecting data on both current and desired performance, you can consider the unique perspectives of those providing data for the needs assessment. If, for example, the needs assessment identifies that trainers in your organization believe that sharing real-time feedback with learners is critical to e-learning success, but the computer technicians view real-time feedback as an optional performance requirement, then these differences should be addressed prior to implementing any performance solutions. A systemic needs assessment will help you identify and resolve these potential conflicts early in the selection, design, and development process.

The identified and prioritized needs (and strengths) from the assessment are essential ingredients in determining the appropriate objectives for a performance improvement effort. By comparing the costs of addressing each gap (i.e., need) with the associated costs of not closing the discrepancies, the needs assessment data can provide a foundation for setting useful performance objectives. [13, 14]

Case in Point

The previous training manager at Pill Containers administered a "training needs assessment" just prior to leaving the position. The training needs assessment team surveyed managers and supervisors in each division of the organization, requesting information on the skill levels of current employees and perspectives on which training programs could be most beneficial to the division. This assessment provided some useful information on the perspectives of managers and supervisors within the organization, and generated a fair amount of excitement around training opportunities within divisions. It didn't, however, offer the performance improvement initiative data for making effective decisions regarding the accomplishment of useful results. In addition, the improvement initiative now had to address the expectations managers and supervisors had for funding the training programs they had requested.

Knowing that information regarding current and required performance was necessary to improve performance, the improvement team decided to conduct a short results-focused needs assessment that would assist them in verifying the alignment of internal and external results. Data from the assessment would also help guide their decisions later on, when they look at possible performance technologies and communicate with divisions about how the selected improvement efforts are expected to be more effective than the requested training programs.

To begin the needs assessment, the team reviewed the strategic planning documents they collected and identified the results that they believe had to be accomplished in order for the organization to be successful in meeting the upcoming demands of their clients and the communities they serve. After identifying the results to be achieved at the societal (i.e., mega), organizational (i.e., macro), and individual/team (i.e., micro) levels, the needs assessment team verified that internal and organizational partners agreed with the targets (as well as performance indicators selected for each result).[15]

Using online surveys and interviews, the performance improvement team quickly captured the perspectives of many colleagues, clients, suppliers, and external partners on the current level of achievement, as well as the desired performance. In addition, the team used the time to collect whatever performance data they could

Case in Point (concluded)

find to supplement the "soft" data. In only a few days, the performance improvement team had a wealth of information on the current
performance and its relationship to future requirements of the
organization. After a brief analysis of the data, the team could then
identify performance gaps, as well as some emerging opportunities
and strengths that they can later capitalize on when creating an
effective solution set of performance technologies.

The Context for Performance Improvement

The analysis of strategic directions provides for the alignment of
long-term goals and objectives among the partners in a performance improvement initiative. The needs assessment then offers
data to support the identification of discrepancies between current
performance and desired performance. To supplement this developing definition of desired performance, use a SWOT analysis
(Strengths, Weaknesses, Opportunities, and Threats) to put forward
a context for improving performance. The information collected
through a SWOT analysis is essential in making improvement decisions; it describes the relationship between where the organization
is today and where it wants to be in the future. Strategic plans and
needs assessment data are commonly included as information
sources in SWOT analyses, allowing the less formal "brainstorming"
processes of the SWOT analysis to help fill in the gaps between
these other essential ingredients to useful decision making.

   The SWOT analysis identifies environmental and operational
factors you'll consider in determining the performance objectives
(and thus the definitions of success) of your performance improvement efforts. As an individual, team, or organizational brainstorming
activity, most SWOT analyses identify strengths as *enhancers* to
desired performance, and weaknesses as *inhibitors* (both within the
control of an organization). Likewise, opportunities are identified as
enhancers to desired performance, while threats are *inhibitors* (both
outside of an organization's control). For example, your strengths
could include employee knowledge, reliable suppliers, and new
technologies, while your threats include new competitors, employee
recruitment, and limited raw materials. Figure 2.6 displays a common format for classifying factors.[16]

Figure 2.6. A conventional SWOT matrix

SWOT Analysis

Strengths	Weaknesses
• • • • •	• • • • •
Opportunities	**Threats**
• • • • •	• • • • •

Building on this, you can enhance SWOT factors by adding data measured on either interval or ratio scales. Unlike nominal data, where SWOT factors are merely named, measures on these scales allow factors to be related and compared. A standard survey rating scale is an example of an interval measure (e.g., rate your satisfaction from 1 to 5). Similarly, length is an example of a ratio scale measure, since it adds a true zero point to the intervals. Data from measures on either scale will strengthen your analysis with independently verifiable data (such as product return rates, fiscal resources, market share, external impact on the surrounding communities, measures of legislative support).[17]

Using data to verify SWOT factors, ask additional questions related to the cost and causality of each. Namely:

- How much is each factor currently and potentially costing my organization, its partners, and society?

- How much control does my organization have over each factor?

Then review perspectives of each identified SWOT factor using the continuums of both internal-to-external and assets-to-liabilities, (see Figure 2.7). These continuums can help you determine which SWOT factors should be fixed immediately, improved upon over time, sustained, and/or monitored.

Figure 2.7. Expanded versions of the SWOT matrix [18, 19]

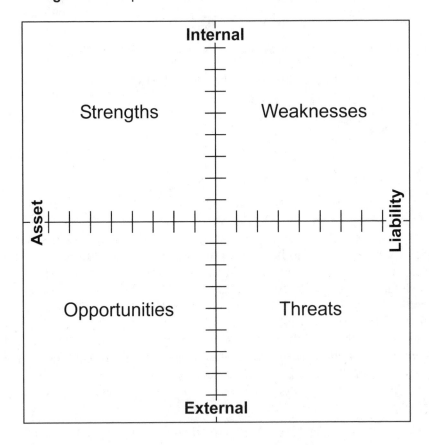

Step Three: Perform a SWOT analysis.

Desired results: A comprehensive analysis of the context for performance improvements.

To begin, identify internal and external stakeholders for the SWOT analysis. These partners should represent an array of business perspectives, such as internal partners from marketing and shipping and external partners like suppliers and clients. The perspective that each partner offers to the analysis provides useful information in determining the appropriate strategic direction for any forthcoming performance initiative.

Next, identify Strengths, Weaknesses, Opportunities, and Threats (SWOT) with the partners. Regardless of the participant characteristics, you will typically want to use focus groups for a SWOT analysis. Either homogenous or heterogeneous groups can be effectively used to generate SWOT data.[20] Focus groups allow for a variety of opinions to be expressed, and you can use structured group processes to facilitate useful dialogue. In most situations, begin your SWOT analysis by asking participants to brainstorm ideas to fit into the following four categories:

Strength: An internal competence, valuable resource, or attribute that an organization can use to exploit opportunities in the external environment

Weakness: An internal lack of a competence, resource, or attribute that an organization requires to perform in the external environment

Opportunity: An external possibility that an organization can pursue or exploit to gain benefit

Threat: An external factor that has the potential to reduce an organization's performance[21]

When you have identified an adequate number of SWOT factors, categorize them into a 2x2 SWOT matrix (refer back to Figure 2.6).

Case in Point

The strategic direction for Pill Containers was becoming evident to the performance improvement team, yet the team still felt as if they were *outside* looking in, rather than *inside* looking out. To help provide a more complete picture of the organization, Landon decided that it would be useful for the performance improvement team and organizational leaders to complete a half-day SWOT exercise. The exercise would aid in defining the context in which the performance improvement initiative will take place.

There were eleven participants: three HR people, four senior managers, three employees from the largest divisions, and one vice president. The morning of the SWOT exercise, Landon divided the participants into three groups. Each table then identified at least four Strengths, four Weaknesses, four Opportunities, and four Threats. After an hour, the groups shared their results, and the participants spent the next hour describing and defining their selections.

With more than two dozen SWOT elements now included in their matrix, the group set about the task of determining which elements were under the control of Pill Containers, and which were under the control of external partners and organizations. For example, the Strength of "experienced employees in manufacturing" was a SWOT component that the organization had control over; the participants quickly realized how this might later shape performance technology solutions related to employee retention. Respectively, the Threat of "external competition in West Coast markets" was a SWOT component that the group recognized was not under their control. The groups also evaluated the SWOT elements along the continuum of being an asset or a liability for the organization.

Although the additional analyses of the SWOT elements took the group longer than they anticipated, all of the participants agreed to work through lunch to finish the exercise. The final task for the group was to prioritize the SWOT components into categories: those the organization should monitor, those that the performance improvement team should work to sustain or improve; and those that the performance improvement initiative should target for fixing or amplifying (see Figure 2.8).

Case in Point (concluded)

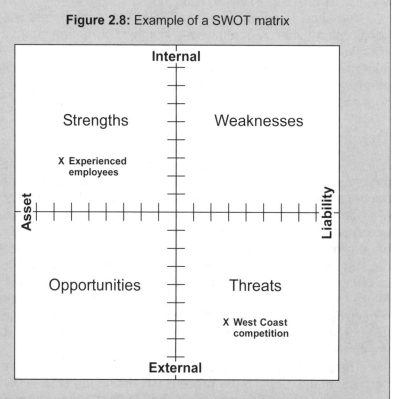

Figure 2.8: Example of a SWOT matrix

Internal

Strengths   Weaknesses

X Experienced
employees

Asset   Liability

Opportunities   Threats

X West Coast
competition

External

With the results of the SWOT analysis, the team could now make important decisions, knowing that their decisions would be anchored in the priorities of the organization and clearly aligned with the performance context.

Identify and associate supporting data (ideally, a combination of hard and soft data at interval and ratio scales of measurement) for each item in the matrix. With additional data, you can then prioritize items identified in the initial brainstorming session to define and describe the relationships that exist between them.

Ask these questions to categorize each factor: (a) To what extent does this item represent an asset or liability to the organization and its partners? (b) To what extent is this item within the control of the organization? Include each item from the brainstorming sessions in the SWOT matrix (refer back to Figure 2.7) based on the responses to these two questions.

You should use data from the SWOT analysis to provide additional information regarding the context of future performance improvement initiatives, and add another valuable ingredient for determining the desired results of your performance improvement efforts. Results of a SWOT analysis can thereby guide your selection, design, and development processes.

Defining Priorities

It is now time to set priorities for your performance improvement initiative. You have completed an analysis of strategic directions, conducted a needs assessment, and facilitated a SWOT analysis, each providing essential information for identifying the results to be accomplished and defining success. At this stage in the improvement process, you are not selecting any performance technologies (i.e., solutions) to achieve the desired results. You are instead focusing on prioritizing performance requirements that will guide future decisions. Set these priorities sequentially at the societal, organizational, and then individual/team levels. This will ensure alignment of any improvements with the desired results at each level.

The priority performance objectives that you establish with your partners at this point in the process will define the criteria on which future evaluations of success can and should be made. If organizational partners later want to judge the success of your performance improvement efforts on other variables, the priorities identified in this step of the process should be reviewed and used to support the many critical decisions that were made in the selection, design, and development of the resulting performance technologies. Judging success on criteria other than those selected to guide the performance improvement process is impractical, since the achievement of other results would be unintentional at best. (Although unintentional results can be beneficial at times, they are not ideal for ensuring the long-term success of organizations.)

Step Four: Set priorities.

Desired results: A prioritized list of performance objectives for the organization and its partners.

Setting priorities among the identified goals, objectives, performance discrepancies, and opportunities can be challenging. The strategic directions of the organization and its partners provide valuable information for aligning performance goals, yet these long-term goals and objectives can lead to struggles when the organizational visions, missions, and performance objectives do not align. While you may struggle to link the performance objectives of internal and external partners, systematically aligning objectives is essential for long-term success. Lead the organizational partners in coming to agreement on the results that each will contribute and how those accomplishments will benefit the society in which they operate.

Use strategic objectives in your needs assessment process to identify both current and desired performance. The results of the needs assessment will provide the necessary details for defining priorities among competing objectives. Gaps between desired (What Should Be) and current (What Is) performance levels add a realistic cost-benefit perspective to decision making. Add the findings of a SWOT analysis to set priorities within the context of the organization's working environment.

It is important that you utilize data from all three of these resources in prioritizing the performance objectives. A structured group technique for building consensus (e.g., Delphi, nominal group technique, social facilitation) is often useful for organizing the competing priorities that will likely exist among organizational partners.

In the end, it is essential for the success of any performance improvement effort to have an agreed upon list of priority performance objectives that can be used to guide decision making. Moving ahead and making decisions without clear agreement on the desired results to be accomplished (i.e., the definition of success) is dangerous and often leads to no useful results or results that take the organization away from its intended objectives.

Chapter Summary

The first step in improving performance focuses on identifying the results that define success. By using a combination of strategic plans, needs assessment, and SWOT analysis results, you can prioritize the accomplishments that are expected from your improvement efforts. In addition, you can guide future decisions by aligning objectives (from all organizational partners) at the societal, organizational, and individual/team levels. These are each necessary steps for ensuring that you have a clear, comprehensive, and specific set of performance criteria on which to base decisions and measure your success. In the next chapter we will translate the desired results into specific performance objectives for both the performance improvement system and the individual performance technologies that are selected for the set of solutions.

Chapter 2 Notes

1. Kaufman, Watkins, and Leigh, 2001

2. Kaufman, 2006

3. See Kaufman (2006) for complete societal vision statement

4. Kaufman, Oakley-Brown, Watkins, and Leigh, 2003

5. Kaufman, Oakley-Brown, Watkins, and Leigh, 2003

6. See Scriven, 1967

7. See Watkins, Leigh, Platt, and Kaufman, 1998

8. See Kaufman, 2006

9. Watkins and Wedman, 2003

10. Watkins and Wedman, 2003

11. Kaufman, Oakley-Brown, Watkins, and Leigh, 2003; Kaufman, 1992, 1998

12. The results of Likert-type scale surveys are often mistakenly thought of as hard data, since they result in quantifiable data. This is a good example of why we should consider data on both dimensions (hard-soft and quantitative-qualitative), since a single dimension might lead to confusion and the use of inappropriate statistical techniques and related conclusions.

13. See Kaufman, 2006 (book 1 of this series)

14. Watkins, Leigh, Foshay, and Kaufman, 1998

15. Kaufman, 2006

16. Leigh, 2006

17. Kaufman, 1992, 1998

18. Leigh, 2006

19. Based on Leigh, 2006

20. Leigh, 2006

21. Capon and Disbury, 2003

Chapter 3
Define Success

Introduction

The definitions of *success* for any performance improvement effort and the related criteria for evaluating success can vary greatly, depending on the individual perspective of the evaluator. Program administrators, initiative sponsors, initiative managers, support staff, presidents, CEOs, workplace supervisors, second-generation clients, and others are each likely to have a unique perspective regarding the results associated with success (and how their objectives should guide your decisions). Criteria for defining success should, therefore, include broad perspectives as you select, design, develop, implement, manage, and evaluate performance improvements.

> *Whatever you can do or dream you can, begin it.*
> *Boldness has genius, power, and magic in it.*
>
> – Johann Wolfgang von Goethe[1]

Most perspectives of success are developed with little data to support their conclusions. Personalities, politics, budgets, personal agendas, and other variables often play an equal or greater role in determining the generalized success of organizational initiatives than do the performance criteria on which programmatic decisions were made. For instance, in many organizations the successful implementation of performance technologies such as quality circles or balanced scorecards are judged on the degree of engagement of organizational leaders or the friendliness of the implementation manager (regardless of the results that are accomplished or their contribution to the organization's strategic objectives).

You have little control over many of these variables, so evaluate the success of your improvement efforts only by the criteria that are agreed to by organizational partners and used to inform decisions during the selection, design, and development processes. Since you have included diverse perspectives in these criteria, they can be used to develop a comprehensive definition of perspectives in these criteria, they can be used to develop a comprehensive definition of success. Perspectives such as those of internal colleagues, clients, clients' clients, and others in our shared society are each valuable in determining the performance objectives that will guide your improvement efforts.

By aligning performance objectives, you can effectively define and communicate the results that should be associated with success. Work with internal and external organizational partners to agree upon a common definition of success: a definition based on the performance objectives that can be used throughout a performance improvement initiative to guide decision making. This is a practical approach to defining success and will divert later conflicts.

> *If you can't define it, you can't improve it.*

A process for defining the performance objectives (i.e., results) that guide your improvement efforts is outlined in this chapter (see Figure 3.1). Use this process to coordinate the formal and informal evaluation of performance improvement efforts with internal and external organizational partners. Evaluate performance improvements only on the performance objectives that you all agree to.

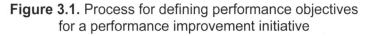

Figure 3.1. Process for defining performance objectives
for a performance improvement initiative

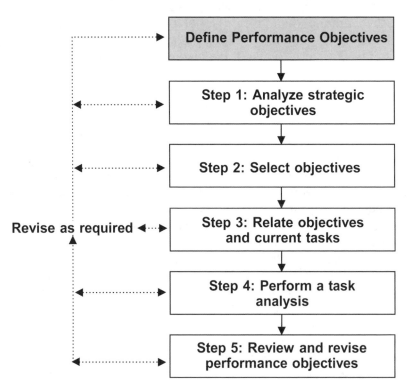

Strategic Analysis

To identify the goals of your organization and its partners, performance expectations at the societal, organizational, and individ-
ual/team levels were previously derived from strategic plans, needs
assessment, and SWOT analysis results (see Chapter Two). As
isolated goal statements or mission objectives, however, the value
of these intended results is limited. For useful results to be
achieved, you will have to identify more-detailed performance
objectives and use them to guide your decisions.

The shared and unique performance requirements of the
organizational partners must now be related to the specific context
of your performance improvement effort to guide decisions related
to the selection, design, and development of useful performance
technologies. An analysis of performance expectations (strategic,

tactical, and operational) is used to link those intentions with the specific results that must be accomplished by your efforts.

For example, "zero safety-related defects" may be a shared objective among the organizational partners (including suppliers, manufacturing, marketing, direct clients, and consumers who later utilize the product). By itself, however, this organizational objective does not provide the necessary guidance for selecting specific performance technologies to be included in the set of solutions. Therefore, you will use the related individual/team objectives (e.g., all team products include a completed inspection checklist for safety-related defects) to provide additional guidance.

Start by again reviewing the shared performance expectations of your organization and its partners. Identify the performance objectives that represent the necessary results to be accomplished for each strategic objective to be realized, at each level. These integrated objectives will define which results must be accomplished by your performance improvement efforts. This also ensures that the products developed within the organization (micro-level results) are supportive of the required client deliverables (macro-level results) and contribute to the long-term success of societal partners (mega-level results).

Step One: Analyze strategic objectives.

Desired results: Document that illustrates the alignment of perform- ance requirements at all three levels of results.

Begin your analysis with performance objectives shared across the organizational partners. Using the strategic objectives identified from the strategic plans, needs assessment, and SWOT resources, identify the shared objectives at the societal level as a starting place. Here the desired results that contribute to the health, safety, well-being, and satisfaction of societal partners are the focus. Ana- lyze each mega-level objective to identify the building-block results that are necessary for the accomplishment of the desired results.

To analyze mega-level objectives, you should ask: *If this shared societal objective is to be accomplished, what results must my organization contribute?*

Many organizational objectives from your previous review will likely align with desired societal contributions. In addition, you may identify several new performance objectives (i.e., desired results) for your organization. These can represent new opportunities and/or characterize new partners that should be explored. (As we mentioned before, if your review of direction-setting documents from your organization and its partners doesn't identify any societal-level objectives, you can either take the time to define those objectives and their relationships now, or make a note that systemic strategic planning is likely a performance technology to be considered later on.)

Organizational objectives are the results of societal analysis. One or more of the necessary results for achieving societal outcomes should be identified in your organization's tactical objectives (thus aligning the outputs of your organization with contributions to the shared societal objectives). This alignment of the organizational objectives is essential for the accomplishment of desired societal contributions and shared success.

From the societal-level analysis you ideally have a robust set of organizational objectives. Organizational objectives must also be analyzed to provide direction to performance improvements. Analyze each of the organization's tactical objectives to determine which results must be contributed by individuals and teams (e.g., performance technologies).

To analyze macro-level objectives, you should ask: *If this organizational objective is to be accomplished, what interim results must be accomplished by individuals and/or teams?*

The identified building-block results are your individual/team (i.e., micro-level) objectives. When you accomplish these individual/team objectives, then organizational objectives are achieved and societal contributions are made. This analysis will typically identify many performance objectives not found in your review of strategic direction-setting documents. You should, however, identify as many individual and/or team objectives as are necessary to achieve organizational objectives.

Take, for example, an organization that manufactures automobile windshields. One of the societal objectives that it shares with its external partners is to contribute to the health and safety of everyone in the community. The interim results the organization delivers to clients should therefore be aligned with this shared objective. By delivering products that reduce the number of passenger fatalities to zero over the next 20 years, the organization is making a direct contribution to the shared societal objective.

Likewise, an analysis of the organizational objective (zero pedestrian fatalities) will identify the individual and team results that must be accomplished for the organization to succeed. A transparent material that provides the necessary visibility without the rigidity of glass, safety reports from leading automobile manufacturers on the functionality and safety of the new material, and/or government approval of a new product may all be objectives for individuals or teams within the organization. This aligns the results produced by individuals and teams with the strategic objectives of the organization (and its partners).

Your performance improvement efforts should target one or more organizational objectives that are aligned with societal benefits. Similarly, each performance technology included in the set of selected solutions should target one or more individual/team objectives. Utilize objectives at all three levels to guide your decisions and determine what results will define your success (see Figure 3.2).

Don't, however, select any performance technologies at this time. Only specify the results that must be accomplished; this ensures that all decisions about "what to do" are aligned with standards for "what has to be accomplished." For now, focus solely on the results to be accomplished, and not how those results may be achieved.

Figure 3.2. The alignment of Mega-, Macro-, and Micro-level objectives with performance technology solutions

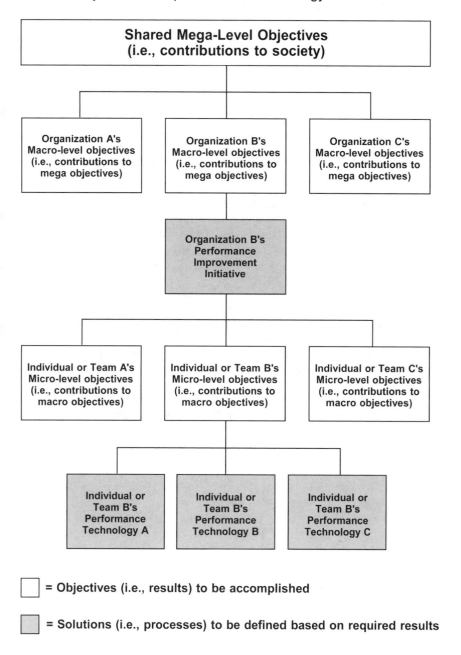

= Objectives (i.e., results) to be accomplished

= Solutions (i.e., processes) to be defined based on required results

Case in Point

Before making any critical decisions regarding the performance improvement initiative, the Pill Containers team wanted to verify the alignment between internal and external results and payoffs and define objectives in enough detail and precision so that any decisions they made would lead to useful results. To do this, they simply categorized the results they now knew would have to be accomplished into the societal, organizational, and individual/team levels. At the societal level, they included the shared results that their organization and its partners (including suppliers, direct clients, indirect clients, and community partners) had previously agreed to as their long-term objectives.

Likewise, at the organizational level, the team included the specific results that Pill Containers would contribute to the shared mega level objectives. At times, the team identified elements of the mega-level objective that neither their organization nor their partners were committed to. These were put into a separate file labeled "Future Opportunities."

Knowing the results that their organization was now committed to delivering to external partners, the performance improvement team next examined the alignment of the internal organizational divisions with the accomplishment of those results. This part of the analysis was more challenging for the team, since many divisions of the organization had not yet clearly identified the products they contribute. With some assistance from both the improvement team and the external partners, the group was able to define the performance contributions from each division of the organization (noting that some divisions would have to change their focus from just doing what they have always done to improving the results they contribute to the organization).

In the end, the improvement team developed a helpful "map" that linked together all elements of the internal organization to what they are contributing to the success of the organization. In addition, they now understood how the internal organizational partners work with and contribute to the success of external partners—all of whom they soon realized would be of great value as they tried to determine which results would be the focus of their improvement efforts.

The analysis of results at all three levels identifies precisely what the performance improvement activities within an organization are supposed to achieve (see Table 3.1). These results provide an essential guide for selecting, designing, and developing useful performance technologies.

Table 3.1. Mega, Macro, and Micro analysis

Analysis	Results
Analysis of Mega-level objectives	Produces detailed organizational (macro-level) objectives for the success of the organization as a whole
Analysis of Macro-level objectives	Results in detailed individual/team (micro-level) objectives for the success of performance improvement initiatives
Analysis of Micro-level objectives	Results in detailed interim performance objectives for the success of performance technology projects

You are not on your own in accomplishing results at all three levels. Internal and external partners can (and should) work together to ensure that all processes and products are resulting in valuable contributions. After all, societal results are not produced or achieved by any single person or organization.

Regularly review the alignment of societal, organizational, and individual/team objectives. You should continually verify which results must be accomplished and link your decisions to those objectives. By doing this, you will also identify new markets, new technologies, and new opportunities to improve.

Performance Objectives

The required results (i.e., performance) identified in the analysis of strategic objectives provides measurable targets. This information tells you where you are headed and how you will know when you have arrived. Clear linkages to the strategic directions of the organization and its partners are also identified through these performance objectives. They should contain the specific results criteria that will guide your decisions without identifying the processes by which those results might be achieved.[2] This will leave all options on the table when it comes time to select appropriate performance technologies.

Detailed objectives for a performance improvement initiative provide specific guidance for making essential decisions about which performance technologies are to be designed and developed. In addition they offer useful criteria for assessing the accomplishments of the initiative before and during implementation. Hence, use a systematic process to select those objectives that will guide your efforts. To achieve of these standards, select aligned performance objectives at all three levels.

Step Two: Select objectives.

Desired results: A list of performance objectives to be accomplished by the performance improvement initiative.

The selected performance objectives define *success* in pragmatic terms. Accomplishment of the agreed upon objectives should be the primary (if not sole) criteria used to assess the achievement of your performance improvement efforts. Use the results from your analysis of strategic objectives to identify what results are to be achieved at all three levels. Also review the results of the needs assessment and SWOT analysis to verify that the selected objectives are aligned with organizational (and partner) priorities. Choose the performance objectives that will guide decisions, and then review those in relation to the scope (e.g., time, resources) of your improvement efforts.

Since perspectives on what results should be accomplished typically vary among internal and external partners, the selection of performance objectives is critical to success. For example, a client's definition of success might have to do with the delivery of no defective products. Alternatively, a supplier's definition of success may be linked to improved supply-chain management. Work closely with organizational partners to gain desired agreement, and be clear with the partners that the future selection of performance technologies will be based on these objectives.[3]

To guide decisions, each of the selected performance objectives should contain detailed descriptions of the results to be accomplished. General goal statements about such things as providing quality customer service or reducing operations costs found in organizational planning documents must often be revised to provide the necessary details. Objectives should include information such as how results will be measured, what standards will be used to define success, and when results are to be accomplished.

Use the objective framework in Table 3.2 as a tool for reviewing and revising objectives. They should clearly communicate what results are to be achieved. When a performance objective doesn't provide the necessary information, work with internal and external partners to adjust the objective prior to making performance improvement decisions. Complete objectives should have all seven characteristics of the framework: They should be specific, measurable, audacious, results-specific, time-bound, expansive, and reviewed.

Table 3.2. Definitions of SMARTER performance objectives[4]

S	The objective must be written for a **Specific** result.
M	Each objective must be observable and therefore assessable. This means that the objective must include a **Measurable** component stated in interval or ratio terms. The objective must answer these questions: How much? How successful? How many? How audacious? How well? How proactive?
A	The objective should aim at significant change, paradigm shifts, or challenges to the status quo. We call these **Audacious** objectives because they challenge individuals, teams, and organizations to stretch their horizons and exceed the present level of results.
R	Each objective must define the **Results** (i.e., performance) to be achieved and exclude the methods and means to achieve the result. In other words, the objective is written for a key result area—not for an increase in activity. The key result areas are at all levels: mega, macro, and micro.
T	Each objective must have a target time for completion. It must be **Time-bound** or refined.
E	The sum total of the objectives are **Expansive** (i.e., they are aligned and supportive of each other—inclusive and linked).
R	Objectives should be evaluated and **Reviewed** to check relevance and progress toward the results.

Case in Point

Pill Container's performance improvement team selected and refined their performance objectives. The selected objectives offered useful criteria for choosing promising performance technologies and valuable evaluation criteria that could later be used to judge the success of the initiative. A sample of the performance objectives include:

Mega-level objectives that are shared with organizational partners:

- In twenty years, and from then forward, zero patients will die or be harmed because they took the wrong prescription medicines, as measured by studies conducted at the National Institutes of Health.

- In fifteen years, and from then forward, workplace injuries and accidents will be reduced to zero, as measured by the Occupational Safety and Health Administration (OSHA).

Macro-level objectives for Pill Containers:

- In fifteen years, and from then forward, zero patients will die or be harmed because they took the wrong prescription medicines (due to confusion or other problems related to the pill container).

- In eight years, and from then forward, no employees at Pill Containers will be injured in workplace accidents, as measured by the organization's annual safety records review.

Micro-level objectives for divisions within Pill Containers:

- In five years, the design division of Pill Containers will develop a new product line that can prevent customer confusion regarding the contents of the product.

- In ten years, the sales division of Pill Containers will secure contracts ensuring that at least 25% of the pharmacies in the United States will be using the "confusion free" containers developed by the company.

- Next year, no divisions of the organization will have a workplace injury, as measured by the annual safety records reviews.

- By next year, the human resource division will establish guidelines for completing an annual safety records review.

Case in Point (concluded)

> • In five years, Pill Containers will provide the professional association of pharmaceutical container manufacturers with guidelines for accident-free operational procedures for use throughout the industry.
>
> These performance objectives identified by the improvement team were based on the strategic plans of the organization and its partners, the needs assessment conducted by the team, and the SWOT analysis that was conducted just a few weeks ago. To gain additional support, the improvement team decided that the company's senior managers and organizational leaders, as well as the external organizational partners, will each have the opportunity to review these performance objectives.
>
> After several meetings with both the internal and external partners, there was agreement that the primary focus of the results to be accomplished were consistent with the strategic goals of Pill Containers and its partners (even if a few details would have to worked out over time). In addition, the senior management team for the organization agreed to review these objectives at their next strategic planning retreat (in the spring), in order to integrate the results into their upcoming planning documents.
>
> With this vote of confidence, Landon and the performance improvement team felt secure that they could base their future decisions on the achievement of these objectives. As an additional benefit, the team also knew that they could use these same objectives to later evaluate the success of selected performance technologies.

Applying Performance Objectives in Context

Your selected performance objectives are based on the results of several planning, assessment, and analysis processes. Each of these processes is focused entirely on results; either current or desired. To identify and select appropriate performance technologies for accomplishing these objectives, consider the current processes of the organization. Current organizational processes provide the context in which present and future results will be achieved.

In a computer supply company, for instance, let's say the analyses identified a requirement for teams within the shipping department to reduce processing time to less than eight hours in order to meet the performance expectations of external partners. There are many performance technologies that can help you accomplish this objective. However, it is important to ground the performance objectives in the current context of the organizational processes before making any decisions. For example, if the shipping department implemented a new performance monitoring system a year ago that improved the quality of their performance but required additional time for shipping orders, an understanding of the current processes in the shipping department would be essential in determining which performance technologies would help accomplish the related performance objectives.

Step Three: Relate objectives and current tasks.

Desired results: A document linking selected performance objectives with current organizational processes.

Relating current processes to the selected performance objectives helps guide the selection, design, and development of useful performance technologies. Using your list of selected performance objectives, identify which objectives have related tasks that are currently contributing results toward their accomplishment.

Orderly analysis of information is essential for systematically improving performance. Use a structured format (see Table 3.4 for an example) to verify the contributions of current organizational processes to the specified performance objectives. Pinpoint imbalances and possible opportunities when performance objectives are not aligned with current processes. These relationships between objectives and activities provide context for future decisions regarding which performance technologies should be included in the set of solutions.

Current processes within an organization will frequently be contributing toward accomplishment of the identified performance objectives. At this time, however, you only want to examine the alignment of current processes with the selected performance objectives, not evaluate their success. During this review, you don't want to get trapped in the details as to why a current process may or may not be contributing the desired results.

Table 3.4. Relating performance objectives with
current organizational processes

Performance Objectives	Are current processes contributing to results?	If yes, which current processes are contributing results?
	❏ Yes ❏ No	
	❏ Yes ❏ No	
	❏ Yes ❏ No	

Analyses of the efficiency and effectiveness of current processes will be included in the next step: task analysis. Current processes that are aligned with selected performance objectives can
then be assessed to determine if they should be amplified or
expanded, revised or modified, monitored or maintained, over-
hauled, or scrapped in order to accomplish desired results, thus
leaving all options for how performance objectives are accomplished available for later decisions.

As you identify current processes, you and other organizational
partners will likely also identify potential performance technologies
(including both revisions to current organizational processes or new
programs). Keep a list of these potential solutions as you move
through the planning, assessment, and analysis steps. Don't commit to any performance technology solutions at this time, but don't
lose track of good ideas either. These options will later be useful in
identifying potential and alternative performance technologies to be
included in the set of solutions.

The premature selection of solutions (such as choosing a new
incentive system or computer software application) prior to fully
defining the results to be accomplished is a path toward disaster,
rather than a path toward the achievement of useful results.

Task Analysis

The selection of useful performance technologies next requires a systematic analysis of the current activities within the organization. Task analysis describes and documents the current processes used by individuals and teams, offering useful insights that inform decisions about how performance can be improved. New performance technologies can then complement or supplement the current activities within the organization and help accomplish valuable results.

Completing a task analysis requires that you get into the often mundane details of the current organizational processes. Take the time to document the specific steps used to accomplish current results. Use a task analysis to detect crucial characteristics for new performance technologies to be successful. As you observe, question, and document the current processes within the organization, routinely identify valuable steps and resources for developing and implementing successful performance technologies. The benefits of systematic task analysis are so valuable, it should be included in any performance improvement effort.

Step Four: Perform a task analysis.

Desired results: A detailed accounting of how current results are being accomplished.

You want detailed information on how current processes are used to achieve results. These detailed descriptions of what tasks are performed, the sequence of events, the processes involved in the completion, and their related results provide essential information for selecting, designing, and developing useful performance technology solutions. Your analysis will both define the process steps being used to accomplish current results and describe the processes that are not achieving results (or that are less efficient than desired). The completed analysis will then help guide decisions about what to do and what not to do.

Start by identifying the tasks associated with the performance objectives you have selected. You may be able to group tasks by related performance objectives to improve the efficiency of the task analysis processes. When you have identified the possible tasks for analysis, prioritize the list based on the significance of the performance objectives and the contribution of the tasks to the achievement results. Most performance objectives benefit from an analysis of their contributing tasks, but resources are rarely available for this type of systemic examination. Based on the resources you have available, determine which priority tasks will be analyzed as part of your performance improvement effort.

For each selected task for analysis, identify the appropriate task analysis technique(s) to be used. There are four basic kinds of task analysis that can be used independently or in combination:

- Hierarchical task analysis
- If and Then task analysis
- Model-based task analysis
- Cognitive task analysis

Hierarchical Task Analysis. This kind of analysis identifies both the component steps of the given task and their hierarchical (or sequential) relationship to one another. When desired results are not being accomplished, use the hierarchical analysis to provide insights into the obstacles preventing success. Equally, when desired results are being accomplished, use the analysis to detail the constructive processes that lead to accomplishment of objectives.

To begin, review, observe, and document each step taken by the performer in completing the task. Verify the appropriate sequence of steps for accomplishing results and identify the resources (e.g., supplies, computers, or other employees) used to complete the task. Routinely, processes will involve steps that cannot be observed. Talk with the individuals or teams that perform selected tasks to identify internal and external behaviors. The Hierarchical Task Analysis usually requires a combination of observation and interviews with expert performers.

For example, a task analysis may show that receptionists complete the following steps in accomplishing a performance objective for the sales office:

1. Check voice mail messages.

2. Take detailed and accurate notes on each voice-mail message.

3. E-mail district sales representatives with voice-mail messages.

4. Copy the sales manager on e-mails going to their sales representatives.

5. Clear phone messages after e-mail messages have been sent.

Depending on the level of detail required for making useful decisions, additional analysis may be done on any single step within the process to identify more-detailed actions taken by the expert performer (for example, steps required to check voice mail messages). The level of detail required for a task analysis varies greatly from initiative to initiative. Balance the desired level of detail for making improvement decisions with the available time and resources.

If and Then Task Analysis. If and Then analysis applies process logic to the determination of the important decision steps in completing a task. When you have multiple decisions to be made in completing a task, this analysis technique can be useful. For example, for the task of using a word processing software application, one decision step might be this:

If a word in the text is underlined in red, then right-click on the word to identify options for revising the spelling of the word.

As tasks gain in complexity, there will be multiple decisions to be made by the performer. The If and Then analysis then becomes an effective technique for identifying and documenting decisions and behaviors that cannot be observed.

Use observations and interviews with expert performers to complete an If and Then analysis. Combinations of methods are also commonly used to identify the constituent steps in completing many complex tasks.

Continuing the example, receptionists in another sales office might identify the following steps for achieving the same performance objective:

1. Check voice-mail messages when you arrive at work. If there are messages, then take detailed notes on each voice mail message.

2. If the voice mail is for a district sales representative, then e-mail the sales representative the contact information and message from the voice mail (and proceed to Step 4).

3. If the voice-mail message is for a manager, then forward the voice mail to the manager using the *8 feature of the phone.

4. Copy (or inform) the sales manager about e-mails going to their sales representatives.

5. If you have completed Steps 2, 3, and 4 for all voice-mail messages, then delete phone messages.

Model-based Task Analysis. You should use model-based analysis when the task being reviewed is vague and/or difficult to define. Since many "soft skills" or professional tasks (e.g., demonstrating leadership, group problem solving) are characterized by their elusive definitions and reliance on situational context, model-based analysis can provide you with essential information for describing how performance objectives get accomplished in these situations. With model-based analysis, you work closely with performers to develop a model or framework for completing the task and then apply the model, even when there are ambiguous guidelines for performing the task.

For example, for the "soft skills" task of mentoring sales office employees, the analysis might reveal the following performance model:

> Describe for the employee the optional techniques that might be used to complete their work. In mentoring the employee, use one or more of the following techniques: use examples of other current and previous employees; have them form a picture in their minds of performing the work at their desk; demonstrate successful performing of the work related tasks; have the employee practice the work steps and provide immediate feedback; and/or suggest additional training opportunities within the organization.

Use interviews (or focus groups) with expert performers to define a model for a task. After a model is developed, expert performers should again review the procedures and options to ensure that it adequately represents a framework for accomplishing desired results. The ability of a model to represent the successful completion of a task is dependent on the flexibility of the model. If your model-based analysis does not result in a flexible framework that can be applied in a variety of contexts, then you will want to review the task using another task analysis technique.

Cognitive Task Analysis. Cognitive analysis methods focus on the psychological processes underlying the competition of a task. Use cognitive analysis whenever complex decisions are required (such as when multiple contributing variables and options must be weighed by the performer) and when there are few observable behaviors. Subtle cues from the performance context and the experience of expert performers are often discovered through this analysis technique.

To begin, identify, cluster, link, and prioritize the critical cognitive decisions that are routine in expert performance. You then diagnose and characterize these decisions based on the techniques used, cues signaling the decision points, and the inferences made as elements of the analysis.[5, 6] It is often helpful to focus on the critical decisions and cognitive processes that separate novices and experts to determine their importance in completing the task.

Expert performers have often internalized or made habitual many of the key decisions that go into performing the related steps within the task. This makes completing a cognitive analysis challenging. Aid expert performers in communicating their cognitive processes by using techniques such as card sorting, process tracing, or concept mapping.

After analyzing the tasks associated with each priority performance objective, review the analyses for opportunities to improve, lessons learned that may benefit other performance solutions, and/or challenges that could be faced during implementation. Use the results to inform your later decisions about how performance technologies can accomplish useful results.

Case in Point

Regina, a project leader from the manufacturing division at Pill Containers and a member of the performance improvement team, was always willing to share pragmatic suggestions whenever the team seemed to lose focus during meetings. One such suggestion came soon after the team identified the performance objectives that would be used to guide the upcoming decisions. Without hesitating, Regina described for the team how her division had already addressed several of the performance objectives through their quality improvement initiative that started last year. The team quickly realized that this was great news, since these efforts within the manufacturing division would offer them the opportunity to see what is already being done to achieve the organization's objectives.

The manufacturing division was immediately selected to be the first unit within the organization to complete a task analysis for their primary operational functions. The analyses of some functions were best achieved through Cognitive Task Analysis methods, while many other functions were analyzed using Hierarchical Analysis or If and Then techniques. Working with employees from both production facilities, the improvement team quickly completed a task analysis for the eight primary operational functions within the division that were linked to selected performance objectives.

For example, an If and Then task analysis was completed on the current procedures for documenting accidents and injuries. The analysis identified twelve steps that are currently used by employees, three job aids (e.g., check lists), and two forms that must be completed. In talking with employees who have reported several accidents in the division, she was able to identify several opportunities for improving the process (each noted by Regina for later use as optional performance technologies).

Building on the experiences of working with the manufacturing division to complete their task analyses, the individual improvement team members were able to complete task analyses for the primary functions of their unique divisions within a short time. The results of the task analyses didn't always include sufficient details for designing and developing specific performance technologies (e.g., job-specific e-learning courses or job aids). Each analysis did, however, prove valuable for informing decisions regarding the current and future alignment performance technology solutions.

Align Performing with Performance

Performance objectives and related task analyses provide critical information for linking performing (i.e., processes) with desired performance (i.e., results). Before moving ahead, you should affirm their alignment. Use the information and data gained through the previous steps to review and revise any misalignments. This is your opportunity to verify that selected performance objectives are adequately linked to the accomplishment of useful results at the societal, organizational, and individual/team levels.

Step Five: Review and revise performance objectives.

Desired results: Verification and agreement on the results to be accomplished.

Using information from the needs assessment, complete, compare, and contrast the six *performance-focused* cells on the Organizational Elements Model matrix (see Figure 3.5). In addition, using the results of the task analysis, identify valuable information for completing the What Is (i.e., current) cells in the *performing-focused* area.

Figure 3.5. Associating performance and performing within the Organizational Elements Model matrix[7]

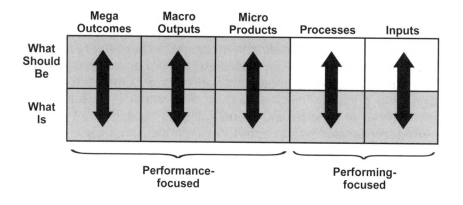

Although you and your partners are likely anxious to identify sets of performance technologies to complete the remaining cells of the matrix (i.e., desired processes and inputs), that step will have to wait until after useful assessments have been defined for evaluating potential technology solutions. For now, identify discrepancies and imbalances between the cells of the Organizational Elements Model matrix and review the associated performance objectives. Sometimes the performance objectives will have to be revised because there is new information. Other times, these discrepancies and imbalances will illustrate opportunities for performance technology solutions.

Many times, the required changes are only minor alterations to the measurement criteria or variations in the timelines associated with each objective. At other times, however, you may identify entire performance objectives that should be either added or deleted from the list.

After making any necessary revisions, verify the updated performance objectives with your organizational partners. These objectives will be used to guide subsequent decisions and should again be agreed upon by everyone. While the organizational partners may have different preferences or perspectives regarding which performance technologies should be used to achieve the desired result, at this point you simply want final agreement on the detailed results you hope for.

Chapter Summary

Performance objectives define in measurable terms the results that must be accomplished by selected performance technologies. Utilize planning, assessment, and analysis documents to define, align, and prioritize these objectives. Performance objectives are best defined in precise and measurable terms and related to the current processes being applied within the organization. Work closely with internal and external partners to secure agreement on goals and results. Rather than relying on assumptions, myths, and other non-systematic processes to guide your decision-making, use the agreed-upon performance objectives as guides for each of the ensuing decisions in selecting, designing, and developing useful performance technologies.

Compared to other processes for improving performance, the Performance by Design approach suggests that an inordinate amount of time and effort is put into defining specific performance objectives. The alignment of all objectives is, however, the only practical way to make sure that your results add meaningful value to the organization and its partners. By carefully defining and agreeing with partners on optimal results early the improvement process, you can better assess the value of alternative performance technologies, select a set of solutions that will accomplish desired results, and relate all design and development decisions to established performance objectives.

Chapter 3 Notes

1. As quoted at http://www.brainquote.com

2. See Brethower, 2005

3. See Brethower, 2005

4. Based on Kaufman, Oakley-Brown, Watkins, and Leigh, 2003

5. Based on http://www.nwlink.com/~donclark/hrd/tasks.html

6. Based on http://www.nwlink.com/~donclark/hrd/tasks.html

7. Based on Kaufman, Oakley-Brown, Watkins, and Leigh, 2003; Kaufman, 1992, 1998, 2006

Chapter 4
Define Performance Assessments

Introduction

Performance objectives are most valuable when they have been defined in measurable performance terms. Before making decisions about how to improve performance, however, you have to identify the actual mechanisms for measuring achievements—that is, the performance assessments that will be used to measure accomplishments. Defining the tools and techniques that will be used to assess performance will help you select appropriate performance technologies (those that can accomplish necessary results), as well as guide any evaluative judgments about the success of the performance improvement efforts. When comparing and selecting alternative interventions, for instance, you will use these measures to assess the potential of each potential performance technology to accomplish desired results.

The process for defining the appropriate performance assessments for each objective includes the identification of the characteristics necessary for an assessment to adequately measure performance, as well as steps for either selecting or creating the necessary performance assessment tools and techniques (see Figure 4.1). You will want to define the performance assessments that will measure your results prior to selecting the performance technologies or processes.

Performance assessments are helpful in a number of ways: they can help you communicate achievements; monitor progress in accomplishing results; clarify results-focused expectations; inform and educate organizational partners; motivate partners; document results; and evaluate accomplishments. That's why they come in a variety of shapes and colors. From single-item data points (e.g., number of products sold) and complex scales (e.g., attitude surveys) to qualitative observations of performance (e.g., task approval) and quantitative comparisons (e.g., balanced scorecards), performance assessments are as diverse as the decisions they support. Be sure that your decisions regarding the selection or creation of assessment objectives are aligned at each level of results.

Figure 4.1. Process for defining performance

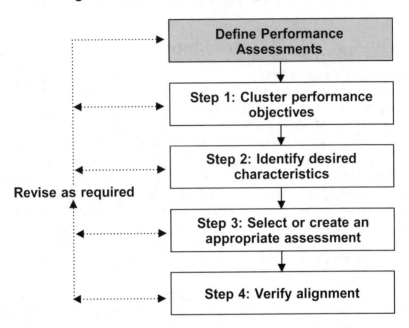

Relating Performance Objectives, Measures, and Indicators

Defining *success* in terms of the results to be accomplished has been our primary focus up to this point. Performance assessments now have to be selected and/or developed to serve as the actual measurement vehicles in determining the success of any selected performance technologies. Do this prior to selecting any perform-ance solutions. The tools and techniques used to evaluate the suc-cess will determine which performance technologies are best able to provide the required results.

Performance measures can be single items of data, aggregates of indicators from multiple components of the same result, or even indexes of data from multiple sources. Most performance assess-ments consist of multiple measures. Depending on the performance objective, a single measure or a variety of measures may be appro-priate. At the individual/team level (where performance objectives are typically most detailed), only a single measure might be neces-sary. It is nonetheless frequently useful to include more than one measure of performance.

Multiple indicators of performance are useful. Measures of workforce compliance, for example, can be combined with a new time-card policy that includes number of users, daily entry logs, number of errors, and so forth. The multiple indicators of performance (i.e., results) can provide a more complete picture of accomplishments.

Each performance objective should have at least one assessment, one measure, and one indicator of performance. When possible, use the same (or similar) measures or indicators to assess results related to more than one performance objective, and try to identify closely related assessments for those performance objectives that are aligned with the achievement of similar results. By increasing the number of indicators and measures of performance, you can improve the accuracy of a performance assessment.

Linking Performance Objectives

Analyze, link, and cluster performance objectives that have related measurements of success to develop effective performance assessments. By doing this, you capitalize on shared measures of performance and reduce redundancies in evaluating success by systemically aligning performance objectives. Review the performance objectives across organizational divisions as well. Look for similarities, associations, sequences, and opportunities to share performance indicators.

It is important to have a systemic perspective of performance objectives (see Figure 4.2). Focusing on single performance objectives can lead to random acts of improvement, rather than a coordinated initiative that consistently accomplishes useful results.

Figure 4.2. Linked perspective of performance

Step One: Cluster performance objectives.

Desired results: A document illustrating the relationships among performance objectives at all three levels.

Use a table (or a concept map) to organize the selected performance objectives at all three levels (see Table 4.1). Organize the objective by their contributions, similarities, shared measures, or sequencing. Complex objectives, especially at the individual/team level, will often be closely related to several other objectives and are likely to be stated in multiple places in the document. The organization of objectives in this manner will help you identify opportunities for aligning or linking performance assessments across multiple objectives.

Table 4.1. Aligning objectives

Societal Objectives	Organizational Objectives	Individual or Team Objectives
Objective 1	Objective 1.1	Objective 1.1.1
		Objective 1.1.2 (and 2.1.2)
	Objective 1.2	Objective 1.2.1
		Objective 1.2.2
		Objective 1.2.3
Objective 2	Objective 2.1	Objective 2.1.1
		Objective 2.1.2 (and 1.1.2)
		Objective 2.1.3 (and 3.4.2 and 6.2.1)
		Objective 2.1.4

Prioritize the clusters of objectives (or single objectives if no clusters are found) based on how critical it is to measure their achievement. You will measure the accomplishment of priority objectives at key milestones throughout the project. Some design milestones, for example, may call for an early assessment of team results (thus getting a higher priority), while objectives related to overall group performance might not be priorities until later in the project (thus getting a lower priority at this time). The clustering and prioritization of performance objectives provides an initial guide for defining the characteristics of useful assessments.

Desirable Traits

Before selecting the actual measures to be used for each objective or cluster of objectives, first describe the necessary characteristics that each assessment should possess. Use a process similar to what you would use when buying a new car (e.g., noting that you desire space, fuel economy, cup holders, and towing capacity). If you start with the desired characteristics, you can make sure that any resulting performance assessments are qualified to assess the performance objectives to which they are associated.

The characteristics that we identify as desirable in a performance assessment tool can provide a clear picture of what we are looking for in our search for options. The desired characteristics should include the ability to measure the necessary results (i.e., validity and reliability) as well as contextual characteristics that will ensure the successful use of the measure within the organization (e.g., budget, time required, necessary data analysis, intrusion on performance environment). These characteristics will determine how we select or develop effective assessments for each performance objective.

Step Two: Identify desired characteristics.

Desired results: A list of assessment characteristics for each performance objective.

For each performance objective or cluster of objectives, starting with the highest priority objectives, determine which characteristics are most important. Only assessments that demonstrate these characteristics will be considered as measures of success. Below are several sample characteristics you may include in your list:

Validity. (How close does the assessment come to measuring the "true" value of what it is intended to measure?)

Reliability. (How often and consistently does the assessment measure the performance and achieve the same results?)

Hard Data. (Does the assessment include indicators of success that can be independently verified?)

Soft Data. (Does the assessment include indicators of success that relate to attitudes, opinions, or contexts?)

Financial Cost. (How much money should be allocated for implementation of the assessment?)

Personnel Cost. (How much time and effort should be allocated for implementation of the assessment?)

Number of Indicators. (How many indicators of performance are desired in the measure? Do they provide a complete assessment of the objective, or will there be a requirement for supplements?)

Partner Agreement. (What level of agreement (e.g., all, most, some) among the partners in the performance improvement initiative is necessary for this assessment to be selected?)

For each performance objective, identify at least two (preferably more) detailed characteristics that are required of any potential performance measures. You will later use these characteristics as criteria for either: (a) evaluating and selecting from optional existing measures or (b) creating unique performance measures specific to the identified objectives. As a result, be sure to identify characteristics in enough detail to guide these decisions.

Case in Point

Before making any critical decisions about which performance technologies will best help Pill Containers achieve its desired results, the improvement team wanted to establish the measures that would be used to judge their success. As a bonus, these measures would also be valuable in selecting performance technologies that meet the requirements of the organization and its many divisions.

The team identified, for instance, two possible performance assessments for the manufacturing division's objective focused on workplace safety. Both assessments were considered to be valid and reliable tools, given the data-collection processes used in each. In addition, both collected some forms of hard and soft data. So what helped the team decide was the time required to complete each assessment. One was an annual assessment that would require twenty to thirty hours of one employee's time to complete each year. The other required multiple employees to conduct focus groups. Each employee would end up spending more than fifty hours on this one assessment. The choice was then obvious, since both provided all the necessary data.

At the same time, the advisory team composed of the company's senior managers and its partner organizations were very supportive of this "planning first" approach to performance improvement. Managers from several divisions within the organization were somewhat concerned, however. Many simply wanted the training they requested the year before, during the training needs assessment. In response, Landon was asked to speak on the performance improvement initiative at several divisional leadership meetings to allay the manager's concerns. The managers seemed mostly concerned about the rumor that the improvement team already had several significant changes in mind for the organization, including a reorganization of divisions that would move staff to the new facilities in the neighboring city.

Case in Point (concluded)

To address these and other concerns, Landon presented the entire Performance by Design framework to the leaders in each of the divisions. He provided detailed information on how the performance objectives for the organization were being identified and prioritized, and described the processes by which performance measures were being used to assess and select from a wide variety of performance technologies. This won the division managers' support, and the performance improvement initiative was transformed from a project within the human resources division into an organization-wide initiative.

After the meetings, leaders from each division provided Landon and his team with valuable input regarding the performance technologies that they believed would best achieve the performance objectives. Without making any assumptions, the improvement team filed the technology suggestions in their growing folder of ideas, letting the divisional representatives know of the performance measures that would be used to assess the benefits and risks of each potential performance intervention.

Choosing Performance Assessments

The next step in the improvement process is to identify assessments that meet the necessary criteria for assessing performance. Use the performance objectives and desired characteristics for each performance assessment as a guide for identifying potential measures of success. Identify at least two potential measures for each performance objective so you have options. (Without options, it is difficult to determine if you have the most appropriate measures.)

Step Three: Select or create assessments.

Desired results: Useful performance assessments for each performance objective or cluster of objectives.

Initially, you only want to identify performance assessments that provide a combination of hard and soft data. Hard data is valuable for providing objective information that is independently verifiable. It is, however, often limited in measuring the attitudes and context in which results are achieved. Soft data is useful for providing information from various perspectives, but it is not independently variable. It is also limited in measuring and relating results across multiple processes. The combination of the two, however, will provide demonstrative evidence to support the assessment of performance objectives and ensure that you are not relying on narrow measures of success.

Also include potential measures that incorporate multiple indicators of performance. For instance, if you want to reduce the amount of time customers spend on the phone with support staff, assessments might be based on data from actual phone records, employee logs, follow-ups with customers, phone-based client satisfaction surveys, and/or performance observations. Within a single measure, such as phone records, identify important indicators such as time on hold, time for initiation to transfer, time from initiation to completion, number of transfers, or time on the phone with the support staff member who actually fulfilled the customers' requirements to get the most accurate picture of the performance accomplishments you can. The identified measures and indicators will provide necessary information for making improvements, as well as evaluating success, so select robust assessments that will provide you with all of the information you think you might want later on.

Sometimes you can only identify one potential measure for a performance objective. In these cases, verify that the single measure meets all of the required characteristics that were previously defined and be sure that the measure includes multiple indicators of performance. Likewise, if you have to create a new assessment in order to measure unique performance, include multiple indicators of performance in the resulting assessment. Single measures with single indicators provide limited information for making important decisions about the successful accomplishment of results or the improvement of performance technologies. Whenever possible, identify numerous robust performance assessments (or create new assessments) that offer multiple measures and indicators of successful performance.

Before selecting any assessments, search for multiple options. Ideally you will identify two or more measures for each performance objective or cluster of objectives. Identifying more options will increase the likelihood that you will find one that can provide all of the essential information for measuring success. (It is often helpful to examine the measures that partner organizations use in verifying their success and/or explore what types of data are available through existing internal quality control systems before you look for options based on the development of new data-collection tools and techniques.)

When two or more options have been identified for each objective or cluster of objectives, evaluate them against your desired characteristics. Not all characteristics will weigh equally in your decision making (for example, financial costs may be a higher priority than the number of indicators), but do assess each option for its ability to meet at least the basic standards of each characteristic you have identified. Use the results of your analysis to prioritize the potential assessments and determine which measures will be of the most value to you in making future decisions and evaluations.

Seek feedback and input from organizational partners prior to making a final selection of performance assessments. These measures will, after all, be used to evaluate the success of the performance technologies included in the set of solutions.

Assessment Alignment

Each selected assessment should be directly related to desired results at the individual, organizational, and societal levels. To confirm the alignment of the performance assessments with objectives, review the complete set of selected assessments to ensure that together they support the necessary measurement of accomplishments at all three levels. Assessed results at the individual/team level should, for instance, relate to results at organizational and societal levels. Confirming the alignment of assessments with the strategic aims of the organization and its partners verifies that performance technologies will be assessed (prior to selection) and evaluated (during development and implementation) with appropriate measures.

Step Four: Verify alignment.

Desired results: A record of linkages between performance assessments and performance objectives (or clusters of objectives).

Starting with the assessments associated with individual and team performance objectives, review each to make sure that it provides you with the necessary information for measuring the accomplishment of the performance objectives. Since a single measure or indicator may be associated with multiple performance objectives, it is important to accurately "map" each objective to its related assessments (see Table 4.2). In reviewing the assessments, identify the clusters of assessments that are multiple objectives.

Table 4.2. Aligning performance assessments
with objectives at each level

Societal Objectives	Organizational Objectives	Individual or Team Objectives	Related Performance Assessments
Objective 1	Objective 1.1	Objective 1.1.1	Assessment 1a
		Objective 1.1.2 (and 2.1.2)	Assessments 1b, 1c, and 1d
	Objective 1.2	Objective 1.2.1	Assessment 1b
		Objective 1.2.2	Assessment 1a
		Objective 1.2.3	Assessment 1e
Objective 2	Objective 2.1	Objective 2.1.1	Assessment 2a
		Objective 2.1.2 (and 1.1.2)	Assessments 1b, 1c, and 1d
		Objective 2.1.3	Assessment 2a
		Objective 2.1.4	Assessment 2a

Each organizational performance objective should also be reviewed to verify the associated measures of success. Although the creation of unique assessments is commonly required at this level, assessments of organizational objectives will also often be comprised of multiple individual/team level measures and indicators. You will want to review each measure to ensure that it adequately assessing the necessary results associated with the organizational performance.

As a final verification, review the societal performance objectives and the associated measures of performance. Adjustments to performance assessments and objectives may have to be made if discrepancies are found at any of the three levels. Revise any objectives or assessments that do not meet the characteristics and criteria previously established for acceptable performance measures.

All performance objectives can and should be measured. The challenge is therefore finding the measures that will work for your organization and its partners. If you make significant changes to either the performance measures or objectives during this process, notify and consult with the internal and external partners. After all, changes to either the objectives or measures are modifications to the intended results and how those results will be assessed.

Case in Point

The performance improvement team at Pill Containers had selected measures for each of the performance objectives they were planning to use to guide their decisions. For example, the success of the improvement efforts within the manufacturing division hinged on achievement of the objective of "Zero injuries due to workplace accidents." This objective was especially critical to evening shift supervisors, who were having trouble keeping enough employees on the floor (a variety of "minor" injuries sidelined people each month). There were several perspectives as to which definitions and measures should be used to determine which afflictions would be classified as injuries.

The improvement team started by reviewing the records of reported injuries over the past five years and additional documents supplied by the employee's union. The team subsequently decided that the most valuable measure for determining if interventions have successfully reduced the number of injuries would be the annual workplace accident report completed by the human resources division. This report was an acceptable measure for both union and organizational representatives, because the data collected for the report was clearly aligned with objectives at each level (and met all of the desired characteristics of the improvement team).

Later on, Landon and his team carefully defined the tools (e.g., surveys, interview protocols) that they would use to measure their success for each performance objective. This was important to selecting interventions that would achieve results on those measures, as well as communicating with the internal and external organizational partners about what results they should expect from the improvement initiative.

Chapter Summary

Effective performance improvement efforts clearly define how each performance objective will be assessed before any performance technologies are selected. The selection of appropriate performance interventions can then be done after you evaluate each optional performance technology against the performance assessments to determine which set of solutions will be most valuable to the organization and its partners. As such, the measures and indicators for each performance objective play an essential role in shaping decisions about which performance technologies will ultimately be selected, designed, and developed.

Section Two:
Improving Performance

In Section One, we identified and defined the results that are to be achieved by successful performance improvement efforts, as well as how those results would be measured. These processes now provide the necessary foundation for selecting, designing, and developing useful sets of performance technologies. Section Two will focus on solutions, processes, and technologies that can help you achieve defined performance objectives.

Figure 5.0. The Performance by Design approach

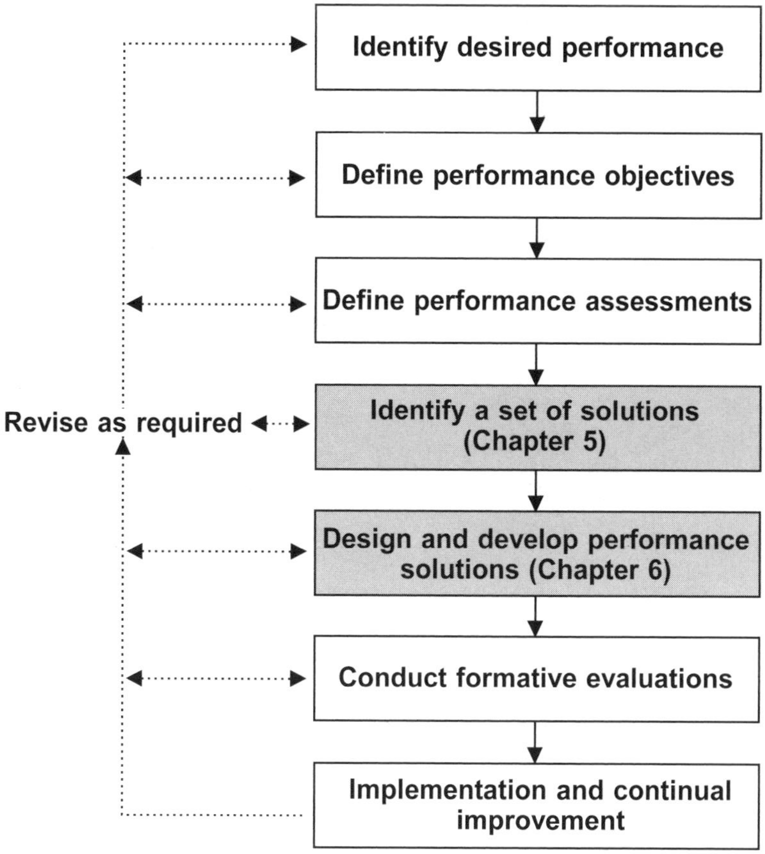

Chapter 5
Identify a Set of Solutions

Introduction

The next step to improving performance is to identify and select which performance technologies are going to accomplish desired results. You begin by looking at the discrete objectives that describe the results required for success, and then use the associated performance assessments to evaluate potential performance technology solutions (see Figure 5.1). This process ensures that the solutions you identify will meet the necessary standards of performance. A performance analysis will then assist you in identifying how multiple performance technologies will be used to accomplish desired results.

Figure 5.1. Process for identifying an appropriate set of solutions

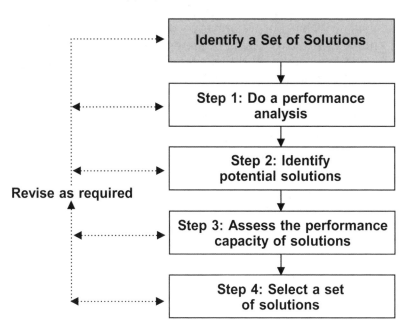

At this point, your focus shifts from the results to be accomplished to the processes and resources that can be used to achieve desired performance. Nevertheless, you will still rely on your performance objectives to guide your decisions and help determine which performance technologies will be of the most value.

Be wary of obstacles to success. These include:

- Informal diagnoses of performance problems (e.g., "The problem is our old computers.")

- Premature selection of solutions (e.g., "Online training will improve our performance.")

- Trendy performance technologies as single solutions (e.g., only electronic performance support tools, only mentoring, only incentive programs, only training seminars)

Each of these can impair the results accomplished up to this point, since they move the focus away from the achievement of results. Most any effort can sometimes improve results (even a broken clock is right twice a day), but to achieve consistent results, base your decision on performance objectives, evaluate potential performance solutions using agreed-upon performance assessments, and focus your efforts on accomplishing useful results at the societal, organizational, individual/team levels.

Analyzing Performance and Performer

Analysis is simply the examination of an element (e.g., a performance objective, a performance discrepancy, a process, a resource) done to determine its contributing factors. In chemistry, analysis provides the researcher with information regarding the chemical composition of a solution; in performance improvement, we examine a variety of contributing factors and their interactions in order to determine which processes can or should contribute to the accomplishment of useful results.

Many approaches to performance analysis only examine factors hindering current performance. For instance, let's say that you identify a discrepancy between the current quality of products being delivered to clients (e.g., 3 in 10 get returned) and the desired quality of products (e.g., only 1 in 1,000 get returned). An analysis of this discrepancy can assist in identifying the factors that are contributing to the disparity in results. The differences between current and required results might have been identified in the needs assessment, though a performance analysis goes one step further to identify (and isolate when possible) the contributing factors that lead to opportunities for performance improvements. Analyzing discrepancies (or problems) is, however, only part of what is required. To improve performance, you must look beyond quick fixes to current problems, failures, or challenges. Instead, use the performance analysis to identify which results must be achieved systemically for desired performance objectives to be accomplished. Instead of looking into the details of current processes to find the one problem that when fixed will improve only isolated components of the performance system, you should explore all of the performance factors that lead to desired results (missing or failing factors can jeopardize success). This process allows you to later identify performance technologies that both address current problems and capitalize on future opportunities.

Performance analysis involves reaching out for several perspectives on a problem or opportunity, determining any and all drivers toward or barriers to successful performance, and proposing a solutions system based on what is learned, not on what is typically done.

— Allison Rossett[1]

The scope and purpose of various approaches to performance analysis vary greatly. Many approaches address performance from an individual performance perspective (e.g., identifying factors that are necessary for individual employees to achieve useful results).[2] Others take an organizational or societal performance perspective (e.g., finding out why the organization is not able to deliver results desired by external clients). Similarly, approaches to analyzing performance problems are diverse in their focus on performing or performance (e.g., learning where the process is failing, versus identifying which interim results are not being achieved).[3] Utilizing identified performance objectives allows you, however, to capture the full array of performance perspectives, as you maintain a focus on useful results at all levels.

Performance analysis is often closely akin to task analysis. It will frequently include the results from previous task analyses to support decisions regarding which performance technologies will be included in a set of solutions. While task analyses focus only on current processes used within the organization to achieve present results, performance analysis examines the processes and inputs necessary for achieving all of the results identified in the performance objectives (see Figure 5.2). A performance analysis can help you define and describe the necessary characteristics of effective performance technologies.

Figure 5.2. The role of performance analysis in the Organizational Elements Model matrix

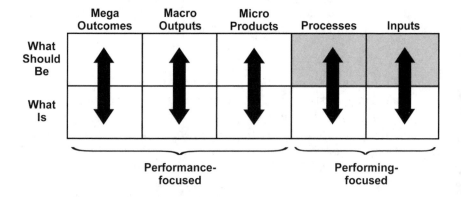

Your performance analysis should focus on factors that will help strengthen or increase results. In doing so, you can identify the contributing factors (e.g., motivation, vision, knowledge, skill) that are necessary for the accomplishment of performance objectives at every level. Many times, a performance analysis suggests that variations of the current processes can achieve necessary results without the addition of new performance technologies. Use the results of prior task analyses to determine how the current processes can be improved.

More often than not, however, identified performance objectives will represent new results to which current processes are not able to contribute sufficient performance. Here, use the performance analysis to identify contributing factors (e.g., expectations, rewards, performance feedback) that are either partially achieved through current processes or that require the development of new performance solutions. If your organization has an underutilized mentoring program, for example, a performance analysis can identify supplemental performance solutions that will assist the program in accomplishing targeted performance objectives. Likewise, the analysis can also identify contributing factors that would benefit from the design and development of new performance technologies.

Successful performance analyses require the support of individual employees who will be responsible for the implementation of any performance technology solutions.[4] Do not try to make these decisions on your own. Include a variety of internal and external organizational partners in the analysis, selection, design, and development processes. From motivation and expectations to self-confidence and perceived capacity to succeed, continually assess the readiness of individuals and teams for the introduction of new performance technologies and other organizational changes. You can assess readiness for change through either informal conversations or formal measures included in performance analysis.

Step One: Do a performance analysis.

Desired results: An accounting of the factors contributing to the successful accomplishment of desired results.

To begin, determine the desired scope of the analysis. Relate decisions regarding the breadth, formality, and duration of the performance analysis to the criticality of the decisions that must be made (i.e., short- and long-term costs and consequences). For instance, a six-week analysis to determine the optimal brand of paper for the office copier is probably a lot more than what is warranted, but a one-day analysis of a million-dollar performance discrepancy in a manufacturing facility is not adequate for useful decision-making. There is, unfortunately, no formula for balancing the competing demands. Simply try to set aside enough time and resources to analyze each of the critical elements that contribute directly to successful achievement of priority performance objectives.

A performance analysis can either be formalized to include the results from extensive simulations, or completed informally through routine observations (when only a limited amount of information is necessary to make decisions). For example, a few years ago a consultant was asked by a fast-food chain to develop on-the-job training materials for several routine employee tasks (e.g., mopping, cleaning windows). By observing employee performance in just two franchises, the consultant quickly realized that there were no gaps in the knowledge or skills of employees related to these tasks. The informal performance analysis indicated that a variety of motivational and performance environment issues were likely responsible for the unacceptable performance levels. The consultant then identified a set of performance technologies that could help accomplish the desired results without extensive employee training. Here an ounce of analysis was worth a pound of training objectives.[5]

Decisions regarding the formality, scope, and duration of each performance analysis should be derived from results to be accomplished. Prioritize which objectives (or clusters of objectives) will be analyzed (and in which order) based on their relative contributions to organizational and societal results.

After developing a balanced plan for managing multiple performance analyses, collect data on factors that contribute to the successful accomplishment of performance objectives. The process should be both systematic and systemic. The Performance Pyramid provides a valuable model for analyzing performance (Figure 5.3).

The Pyramid model illustrates how to design a comprehensive performance analysis. All "blocks" (or contributing factors) within the pyramid must be identified and analyzed for the role they play in accomplishing results. In completing a performance analysis, for example, you should specifically assess the tools and resources provided to organizational teams to determine if they are sufficient to accomplish the required results, as well as survey individual team members to identify potential conflicts between the performance expectations that have been communicated and the feedback they receive regarding current performance.

Use this model to structure the performance analysis and identify the contributing factors necessary for success. Collect data regarding each factor, regardless of related performance solutions. In addition, examine both the current organizational processes that address the contributing factors (e.g., training, strategic planning, incentives, balanced scorecards) and the opportunities to supplement current efforts with new performance solutions.

Figure 5.3. The Performance Pyramid showing societal, organizational, and individual/team foundations[6]

Start your analysis with the contributing factors that provide the foundation for performance: vision, mission, and objectives. Then work your way to the top of the pyramid, including analyses of organizational processes related to each of the contributing factors. Organizations commonly have programs and projects already in place for many of the contributing factors for performance. Review current efforts to assess their capacity to both accomplish desired results and work in concert with other performance solutions. Often performance improvement efforts will focus on enhancing the capacity of these current programs to accomplish necessary results.

Also identify gaps where contributing factors to performance are not being addressed by current organizational processes (e.g., performance capacity, motivation, and self-concept). Blocks in the pyramid that are not attended to by your organization (or its partners) are opportunities to improve performance. In these cases, new sets of performance solutions can complete the pyramid and ensure that all critical factors leading to desired performance are included in systemic improvement efforts.

Table 5.1 illustrates a sample format for organizing performance analysis information. Analyze the unique role each contributing factor plays in the achievement of desired results, but keep in
mind that all contributing factors are usually required. Their relative
contributions, interactions, and prioritization will vary to some
extent, nonetheless, depending on the performance objective.

Table 5.1. Structuring performance analysis information

Performance Objectives	Contributing Factors to Success	Current Contributions
Objective A	Societal vision	No clear linkage to performance objective
	Organizational mission	No clear linkage to performance objective
	Individual and team objectives	Not available at the individual/team level
	Rewards, Recognition, and Awards	No current programs
	Expectations and Feedback	Limited to annual performance reviews
	Tools, Environment, and Processes	Outdated but working
	Performance capacity	New hiring process going into effect this Fall
	Motivation and Self-Concept	Effective mentoring program is in place
	Competence: Knowledge and Skill	Limited training is available
Objective B	Tools, Environment, and Processes	Current processes are inefficient

Apply a combination of data-collection techniques (including
focus groups, individual interviews, and/or questionnaire research)
to analyze the underlying contributing factors necessary to achieve
results. For example, for the team objective of producing a quality
marketing campaign, you would want to assess each block of the
pyramid to determine how each factor will contribute to your
success.

Use performance data to describe the relative contributions and relationships among the blocks. Hard performance data typically comes from automated processes, performance observations, and product quality reviews that can be externally verified. Use it with soft data from surveys, performance ratings, and unsubstantiated performance diaries to derive conclusions and recommendations.

After collecting and analyzing performance data, identify and prioritize the leading factors that contribute to the successful accomplishment of each performance objective. As in prior steps, you will want to examine the factors for redundancies and opportunities so you can capitalize on closely associated contributing factors across multiple objectives. There are, however, no formulas for prioritizing contributing factors. Examine the performance data carefully, work closely with internal and external partners, challenge assumptions, maintain a focus on desired results, and develop your own systematic process for arranging the factors.

It is often tempting at this point in the process to reduce your perspective of performance to faltering processes (i.e., only looking for the "causes" of performance discrepancies). This is not, however, a complete perspective for a systemic performance analysis. Study each contributing factor (i.e., block within the pyramid) to gain a broad perspective on what is required for success. *You must look beyond the problems to find the opportunities.*

For instance, if your organization is not accomplishing a manufacturing objective, searching for a single missing factor is not enough. Fixing or patching just one aspect of a performance system will not accomplish desired results at all levels. Rather, analyze data for all blocks in the pyramid and develop a systemic performance improvement initiative that addresses all shortcomings and capitalizes on current successes.

Even when a manager confidently tells you the cause of the performance discrepancies or their desired solution, continue the performance analysis to identify the other factors that are likely being overlooked. At worse, you will collect data that verifies the perceptions of the manager. More often than not, however, you will determine that the "cause" or "solution" they identified is just one of many contributing factors or possible options for improving performance.

Case in Point

A performance analysis was conducted for every performance priority at Pill Containers. The team used focus groups and performance data from current practices to inform their analysis for most objectives. The team members also concluded that several objectives represented a significant shift from the traditional goals of the organization. For these objectives, employees at partner organizations or other businesses in the area that have similar performance objectives were interviewed.

The company's sales and marketing division, for example, had never identified client satisfaction (when measured by referral rate and repurchase assessments) as a primary performance objective for their organization. They usually focused their goals on new client purchases. The team determined that additional information beyond that which representatives from the sales and marketing division could provide would be necessary to make pragmatic decisions. Information from partner organizations that document performance in terms of past client satisfaction was collected to broaden the perspective of the performance analysis.

The improvement team then completed an analysis of each performance objective, and then prioritized the "blocks" from the performance pyramid model that would contribute to the successful accomplishment of each. These contributing factors for each performance objective provided a framework that the team used to identify which current practices were meeting performance standards (e.g., competence of employee; tools; environment; and processes), as well as areas where new performance technology interventions will have the greatest impact (e.g., individual and team objectives; rewards, recognition, and incentives).

During a performance analysis of the workplace safety objective within the manufacturing division, the team determined that all contributing factors of the pyramid model would make valuable contributions to its accomplishment. The performance analysis results then identified the relationship of each contributing factor to the achievement of the performance objective.

Case in Point (concluded)

Performance Analysis: Conclusions

Skills and Knowledge
Employees are not as knowledgeable as they should be regarding safety issues in the workplace, nor as skilled at making improvements. Improvements in both are essential to the accomplishment of the performance objective.

Tools, Environment, and Processes
Several areas of the manufacturing division are dangerous and should be redesigned for safety. There are, however, no current projects within the organization to make these important changes.

Motivation and Self-Concept
Employees must be more confident in their abilities to improve safety and react when there is accident if the objective is to be achieved.

Performance Capacity
With additional capacity within the workplace (e.g., resources and skilled employees), the number of accidents can be reduced.

Expectations and Feedback
Workplace safety is an important expectation that should be evaluated regularly in order to accomplish the performance objective. Current processes for providing employees with feedback on their safety performance should also be more routine and systematic.

Strategic, Tactical, and Operational Objectives
Safety should be an integral part of all future planning at Pill Containers.

Rewards, Recognitions, and Incentives
Additional recognition of employees who improve safety can help accomplish desired objectives.

Finding Options and Opportunities

The performance objectives, the assessments, and the results of the performance analysis together provide the criteria by which alternative performance technologies can be evaluated and selected. To identify potential performance technologies, look for processes, tools, techniques, or resources that (a) accomplish the useful results defined in the performance objectives, (b) achieve the necessary results as measured by the performance assessment, and (c) address each of the contributing factors required for success.

Review the current literature in fields such as performance improvement, organizational management, computer science, psychology, human resource management, and other associated disciplines to identify possible performance solutions at this point. No options achieving desired results should be overlooked.

Try to find multiple performance technologies (e.g., motivation systems, process redesign techniques, incentive programs, updated software tools, recruitment procedures, strategic planning frameworks) from which you can select the appropriate set of solutions for meeting identified performance objectives. Identify several performance technology options for each contributing factor of each performance objective. Your list of potential performance technologies should be quite long, since each performance objective will have multiple options. You will, however, benefit from having so many options when you are ready to evaluate their capacity to improve performance and select those that will be implemented.

This is the time to solicit creative ideas and preferred solutions from your organizational partners as well. They will undoubtedly be anxious to share their ideas for how to improve performance. From new computer systems and new training programs to expanded incentives and the configuration of workspaces, listen to all their ideas, and make note of each suggestion someone offers. Now is also the time to revive and review the many possible solutions offered during the previous steps of the improvement process. Go over your notes from the needs assessment and SWOT analysis, since these will often include valuable ideas for how performance can be improved.

Step Two: Identify potential solutions.

Desired results: An expansive and comprehensive list of potential performance solutions for each performance objective or cluster of objectives.

Identify a broad list of potential interventions. From leadership seminars and revised performance reviews to workforce retention programs and career counseling, there are a variety of performance technology solutions that can be used to accomplish any desired result. Be sure to identify several solution options for each contributing factor of each performance objective.

Time and again, organizations end up returning to the same processes they have used previously. Training, for instance, is an overused performance technology for many organizations. It is estimated that less than 10 percent of what is taught in conventional training is applied in the workplace.[7] (A similar fate also awaits most any other single-solution performance improvement effort, since the complex systems within organizations are rarely significantly improved by alterations to a single contributing factor.) Use data from the performance analysis to expand your organization's perspective on how varied and combined performance technologies can accomplish useful results.

Use the Performance Pyramid to identify the contributing factors required for successful improvement, as well as to examine the relationships among these essential elements (see Figure 5.4). For each block within the pyramid model, identify the multiple performance technology interventions that might be of value. Resist the tendency to only select from solutions that are well known and/or comfortable.

A variety of performance technologies can assist organizations in achieving useful results at the individual/team, organizational, and societal levels. Potential solutions (i.e., performance technologies) should be linked to the contributing factors identified in the performance analysis. Optional technologies can then be evaluated and prioritized based on their capacity to accomplish the related performance objectives. The solutions that best align with all three (i.e., performance objectives, performance assessments, contributing factors) should then be explored for their likely return-on-investment, while those that do not align well can be removed from consideration.

Figure 5.4. Performance Pyramid, with sample performance technology interventions for each contributing factor[8]

Skills and Knowledge

Classroom training, job aids, e-learning, mentoring, just-in-time training, after-work educational opportunities, knowledge management, etc.

Motivation and Self-Concept

Mentoring, career counseling, motivation workshops, team building programs, etc.

Performance Capacity

Recruitment programs, retention programs, resource allocations, workforce planning, new computer technologies, etc.

Expectations and Feedback

Communication opportunities at retreats and round-tables, performance reviews, balanced score-cards, participation in strategic planning, etc.

Tools, Environment, and Processes

Computer systems, workplace redesign, process re-engineering, ergonimics review, communications, etc.

Rewards, Recognition, and Incentives

Awards program, communications, monetary incentives, performance reviews, balanced score-card, etc.

Strategic, tactical, and operational directions (including vision for community and society; organizational mission objective; and individual and team objectives)

Collaborative strategic planning, needs assessments, balanced scorecards, communication opportunities at retreats and roundtables, etc.

Identify a set of solutions for each performance objective or cluster of objectives. Keep in mind that a single performance technology intervention may address several contributing factors identified in the performance analysis (e.g., a new computer system may help contribute to success in two areas: tools, environment, and processes, as well as performance capacity). The same technology might also be useful for multiple performance objectives. Take a systemic perspective of performance.

When all blocks of the pyramid model are filled and aligned, you maximize the results. Do not expect an ad hoc team to produce a comprehensive review of the current appraisal system if you fail to provide them with each of the foundation blocks in the model (e.g., appropriate tools and processes, performance expectations and feedback, and motives linked to organizational objectives). Instead, make sure that performance technologies targeting all contributing factors are included in the set of solutions. Use the pyramid to (a) prioritize the contributing factors, (b) identify new or revised performance solutions, and (c) determine the appropriate alignment among organizational processes (see Table 5.2).

Table 5.2. Aligning performance technology solutions
with performance objectives

Performance Objectives	Contributing Factors to Success	Potential Performance Technologies
Objective A	Competence: Knowledge and Skill	E-learning Job aids After-work educational programs
	Expectations and Feedback	Balanced scorecard initiative Quarterly performance reviews
	Motivation and Self-Concept	Mentoring Career Counseling

When we limit our options by only identifying one possible solution (or when we push for our favorite solution over other potential options), we lose our focus on results and limit our success. It is by means of this competition among alternative performance technologies that you can identify and select those that will accomplish useful results.

Case in Point

Each member of the performance improvement team was anxiously awaiting the stage in the project when they would be able to decide on solutions. For example, Stan from the accounting division was interested in implementing a new mentoring program throughout several divisions. At first, he believed that mentoring programs could resolve many of the company's problems, but after the performance analysis of each objective, he realized that mentoring was appropriate for only two objectives (with competence and motivation being contributing factors).

The improvement team brought to their next meeting the lists of potential performance technologies they had been keeping, as well as the many ideas that had been shared by internal and external partners. From new interview procedures and online tutorials to monetary incentives and balanced scorecards, the range of potential solutions for each of the performance objectives was broad and impressive.

The team aligned each of the proposed performance technologies with one or more contributing factors and performance objectives. From this the team quickly identified the ones that would be of the most value and the ones that were not solutions to known problems. Many performance solutions were linked to several performance objectives across multiple divisions within the organization. This provided the improvement team with exciting opportunities to implement organizational improvements while working with the enthusiastic representatives of the individual divisions that supported the inclusion of the specific technology within the set of solutions.

What follows are performance technologies identified for each contributing factor from the performance analysis within the manufacturing division (see previous Case in Point for sample results from the performance analysis).

Case in Point (concluded)

Performance Technology Options

Skills and Knowledge
Possible technologies: Improved knowledge management, classroom training, and/or job aids.

Tools, Environment, and Processes
Possible technologies: Buy heart defibrillators and safety kits, and/or redesign dangerous areas manufacturing facilities.

Motivation and Self-Concept
Possible technologies: Revise mentoring program and/or safety training.

Performance Capacity
Possible technologies: Additional resources for safety equipment and/or recruit new employees with life-saving skills.

Expectations and Feedback
Possible technologies: Routine safety performance reviews, safety-focused balanced scorecards, and/or monthly safety luncheons.

Strategic, Tactical, and Operation Objectives
Possible technologies: Systemic strategic planning and balanced scorecards.

Rewards, Recognitions, and Incentives
Possible technologies: Safety awards program each year, and/or incentives for safety improvements.

Evaluating Options

In the end, you should only select a limited number of performance interventions. This selection might seem daunting, given the robust list you have created for each performance objective (and each contributing factor). Remember, however, that the process for evaluating the alternative options is based on the criteria you already established when you defined the performance objectives, identified the performance assessments, and aligned contributing factors. Use these criteria, standards, and measures for each performance objective or cluster of objectives and you'll see that the evaluation process is quite systematic and straightforward. Sometimes there are difficult and "political" decisions to be made. Internal and external organization partners might, for instance, question why their favorite solutions were not part of the improvement effort. Utilize the planning, assessment, and analysis results from each of the previous steps to justify your selections. Data and systematic processes will help you defend the set of selected performance technologies and gain vital support for the accomplishment of useful results.

Step Three: Assess the performance capacity of solutions.

Desired Results: Evaluation report of each potential performance technology using criteria and standards from performance objectives and assessments.

Only those interventions that can help you meet the performance standards identified in the related performance objectives (or cluster of objectives) should be considered. This first-level filter of capacity will help you trim the list of options to just those that can provide adequate results. Study each potential technology, identifying the results that they should be able to accomplish within your organization.[9]

Often you can benefit from the experiences of other organizations. Performance data from internal and external partners can be particularly valuable in making these estimations. However, when performance expectations can't be calculated for a given performance technology, you should also include that as an important comparison factor when assessing it against other options.

Additionally, use the information gained from earlier steps as essential guides for determining which solutions are going to best meet the various performance objectives. Examine each potential performance technology for its alignment with the other contributing factors identified in the performance analysis. One method for doing this is to identify the "active ingredients" in each performance technology intervention in order to define which processes are essential for accomplishing the desired results.[10] Add the results of the SWOT analysis to further determine which option can best accomplish results within the organization's context (e.g., budget, time frame, available personnel resources, current processes).

When exploring the feasibility of solutions, estimate the return-on-investment of each intervention (i.e., costs and consequences). Although actual financial figures are often difficult to calculate before the implementation of a performance technology, even rough estimates can be very useful in guiding decisions.[11] The performance technologies being considered for implementation, individually and together, should be evaluated carefully to ensure the successful achievement of results at the individual/team, organizational, and societal levels.

Case in Point

Evaluating potential solutions (matched to distinct performance objectives) was easier than Landon and the others had anticipated. Implementations of systemic projects like this were usually stymied by the company's internal politics. In the case of this performance improvement initiative, however, many roadblocks to evaluating and selecting the appropriate performance technologies for the solution set had already been addressed. The precise definitions of results to be accomplished and specific techniques that would be used to measure those results gave the team their criteria by which each performance technology would be judged.

For example, when the team discussed the implementation of the mentoring program that was initially supported by the accounting division, it used criteria that had already been identified in the performance objectives and assessments. In this case, the mentoring program appeared to be a very capable performance technology for accomplishing many of the results that were defined within the related objectives. The improvement team was initially concerned about having to fight political battles, but the evaluation process went smoothly because it was based on established and accepted criteria.

Choosing the Appropriate Performance Technologies

Use the evaluation results to select which performance technologies will be part of your set of solutions. It is important to rely on the justifiable support you have from the systematic improvement process in making the final decisions. Review the products of previous tasks to quickly identify and justify decisions regarding which performance technology interventions will be included in the set of solutions.

Be sure you have the support of internal and external partners before you make any organization-wide announcements about the selected performance interventions. At this point in the process, your partners in the initiative should be very well informed about what has been done and why performance solutions were selected; making sure that internal and external partners are your allies. Let them champion the aspects of the initiative that affect their represented division or organization and help guide the individual interventions to the achievement of useful results. The internal and external partners who have participated in the decision-making throughout the process can also mitigate any political pressure to influence your decisions.

Step Four: Select a set of solutions.

Desired results: A comprehensive list of systemic performance technologies to be designed, developed, and implemented.

Single performance interventions can't address each of the contributing factors to performance and accomplish all of the necessary results for most organizations. You should work with your organizational partners to select solutions that will best accomplish the defined objectives for the performance improvement effort. Often this process requires some level of compromise among the partners, since priorities will have to be established.

When selecting solutions, be sure that the selected combination of performance technologies will work in combination to accomplish the required results (and not contribute to performance problems in other parts of the organization). Suboptimization (i.e., the improvement of performance in one subsystem, at the expense of performance in other subsystems or the system as a whole) is always a threat when selecting performance technologies. The only guard you can take against it is to select a systemic set of performance interventions that align with performance objectives at societal, organizational, and individual/team levels. Table 5.3 illustrates a sample format for organizing solutions.

Table 5.3. Format for defining selected solutions

Performance Objectives	Contributing Factors to Success	Selected Solution Set
Objective A	Competence: Knowledge and Skill	E-learning Job aids
	Expectations and Feedback	Quarterly roundtable discussions Quarterly performance reviews
	Motivation and Self-Concept	Mentoring

Case in Point

After reviewing and evaluating each of the potential performance technology interventions, the improvement team selected approximately a dozen solutions to be part the improvement initiative. Each of the selected performance technologies was closely aligned with contributing factors to one or more high priority performance objectives. Two-thirds of the selected technology interventions were also those that benefited multiple divisions within the organization.

Performance technologies selected for the improvement effort included, for example, a new knowledge management system to be used throughout the organization, five distinct workplace redesign projects in separate divisions, a revision of the company's mentoring program, as well as a new effort to recruit, hire, and retain employees with valuable capacity to achieve performance objectives at all levels.

A short presentation highlighting the efforts and decisions of the performance improvement team was then created and delivered to representatives of all of the internal and external partners. The improvement team members each championed one or more specific performance interventions, introducing the performance technologies to associated divisions and organizational partners in order to gain their support for the design, development, and implementation

Case in Point (concluded)

efforts. The support that each member of the improvement team received for the initiative was quite exciting, motivating the team as they transitioned from planning to design and development.

Chapter Summary

Performance interventions must be aligned with those factors that are known to contribute to achievement of useful results. The performance analysis offers a systematic process that helps define those necessary elements for performance and identify optional interventions for each. From balanced scorecards to online training programs, the performance technologies that are likely to produce useful results can then be identified, evaluated, compared, and prioritized using grounded criteria and standards established for each performance objective.

This systematic process for identifying options and evaluating their potential effort is an essential step in the achievement of useful results. Design and development of performance technologies based on assumptions, organizational politics, and/or "favorite" solutions is never advisable. These non-systematic processes reduce the odds of achieving desired results on a consistent basis. The time and effort invested in a systematic selection process will justify your decisions and improve results.

Chapter 5 Notes

1. Rossett, 1999, p. 13

2. Gerson, 2006

3. Rossett, 1987, 1999; Kaufman, Oakley-Brown, Watkins, and Leigh, 2001; Robinson and Robinson, 1995; Gilbert, 1978; Mager and Pipe, 1997; Witkin and Altschuld, 1995

4. Gerson, 2006

5. Harless, 1975

6. Watkins and Wedman, 2003; Gilbert, 1978

7. Stolovich, 2000

8. Wedman and Graham, 1998; Wedman and Diggs, 1999

9. Kaufman, Watkins, and Leigh, 2001

10. See Clark and Estes, 2002

11. See Kaufman, 2006; Kaufman, Watkins, and Leigh, 2001; Kaufman, Watkins, and Sims, 1997; Graham, Wedman, Tanner, and Monahan, 1998

Chapter 6
Design and Develop
Performance Solutions

Introduction

The selection of performance technologies only provides a blueprint for improving performance. Performance interventions have to be designed and developed (and later implemented) for useful results to be accomplished. While these processes are often unique to organizations, there are several principles and steps that can lead to their success.

The tasks associated with designing and developing performance solutions build on the results of the previous processes. Findings from your performance, task, SWOT analyses, and needs assessment will help you make useful performance improvements. You can further improve efficiencies by capitalizing on the common components among diverse performance technologies.

This book is not intended to be a source of specific guidance on the technical aspects of developing any single performance technology (e.g., the steps for creating online animated tutorials or for setting up an incentive system). There are literally hundreds of performance technologies available to organizations, and many have specific development processes based on their technological requirements. The process outlined in this chapter, instead, establishes an all-purpose framework you can use for design and development of most any performance technology (see Figure 6.1).

The introduction of performance technologies will require organizational change. In preparation, develop a management plan that relates the results of planning, assessment, and analysis to the implementation requirements of those tasked with accomplishing useful results.[1] Individuals within your organization must support and be committed to the initiative if improvement results are going to be sustained over the long term.

Figure 6.1. Process for designing and developing performance solutions

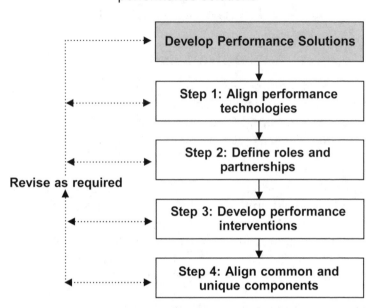

Random Acts of Improvement

We have talked a lot about alignment, but coordination is equally important. Coordination of performance technologies ensures that all performance objectives are being addressed, all contributing factors are being responded to, and all technology interventions are capitalizing on the efforts of other improvement efforts to maximize efficiency and effectiveness.

Try not to make random improvements when designing and developing performance technologies. Performance technologies must work together and with current organizational practices and interventions for improvement efforts to be successful. Use systemic and systematic processes to develop coordinated solutions that accomplish sustainable results.

Step One: Align performance technologies.

Desired results: A report describing or illustrating the relationships among the performance solutions.

Begin with the results of your performance analysis. These results document (or illustrate) the intended alignment of performance solutions with performance objectives (see Figure 6.2). If performance interventions have changed during the selection process, update the results of your performance analysis before making any design decisions. Adding or dropping performance technologies could influence the outcome.

Figure 6.2. Map of performance objectives and the related contributing factors and performance interventions

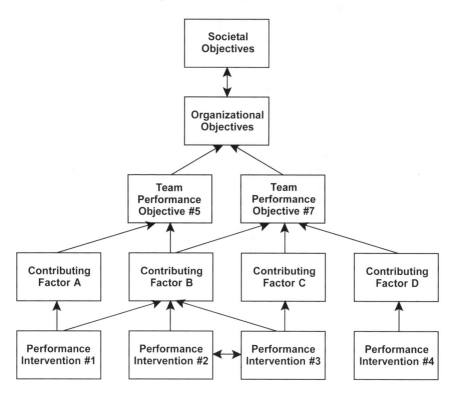

After updating the results of the performance analysis, identify any relationships (e.g., common components, mutual development tasks, similar performance objectives) shared among the performance solutions. Identify possible redundancies or gaps among the selected solutions that might lead to less-than-desired accomplishments. Also look for ways to capitalize on commonalities to improve the efficiency of your design and development efforts. For example, both a motivational workshop and a rewards program may benefit equally from the shared results of a multi-purpose employee questionnaire if the survey process is collaborative.

Just as you clustered performance objectives during the performance analysis, you can also cluster performance interventions based on their commonalities. Group the performance technologies around commonalities (such as shared performance measures, similar participant groups, comparable timelines for implementation, mutual advocates from partner organizations, related design processes, or common development steps). Use these clusters to develop a comprehensive management plan for the coordinated design and development of all new (or to-be-revised) performance technologies included in the set of selected solutions.

Partnerships in Development

Broad-based cooperation is essential to improving performance. The commitment and related tasks of individual partners should be defined and agreed upon for all steps in performance improvement: planning, design, development, and implementation. You do not want to be in the middle of the development process when you learn that a critical team member is committed to the project only through the end of the fiscal quarter or that he or she is being shifted over to another project.

Early on, be sure to define the roles and responsibilities of each partner in the design and development process. Since partners will be assigned to different performance technology projects, identify functional roles and responsibilities for each intervention (or cluster of interventions). Also, provide specific guidance for how each partner and team will work together to accomplish defined results.

Step Two: Define roles and responsibilities.

Desired results: Documentation of the roles and responsibilities each partner has in the design, development, and implementation processes.

Identify the key roles (and related responsibilities) for the design and development of each performance technology. Bear in mind that it is important to clearly communicate your expectations with each partner. As the design and development efforts progress, these roles will expand and contract. Avoid overly general roles that don't align with apparent responsibilities, as they can cause later confusion. Verifying that everyone has a clear understanding of their commitment and your expectation is the key to this step in improving performance. Table 6.1 describes several common roles and related responsibilities that you can use in the development of various performance technologies.

Many common project roles (e.g., initiative leader, improvement advocates, project managers) are required for most design and development efforts. There are, however, several unique aspects to each performance technology that will require the expertise of specialists. For example, to construct a mentoring program that focuses on employee motivation (a necessary contributing factor to one or more performance objectives), the design and development team will require at least one partner who has extensive experience implementing programs that cut across multiple levels of an organization. If, however, you are developing a complementary software system to accomplish results within the same performance objectives, you might find someone with software development or other expertise to aid in the design and development processes.

Work with your internal and external partners to identify and agree upon the related roles and responsibilities for each performance technology. Individuals and the team must then commit to deliver the associated results. When possible, and throughout the improvement process, review the roles and responsibilities assigned to individuals and teams in order to identify possible redundancies or opportunities to capitalize on similar tasks across multiple design and development projects.

Table 6.1. Common roles and responsibilities necessary
for the design and development of performance technologies

Common Roles	Related Responsibilities
Leader of the Performance Improvement Initiative	• Oversees the design and development of multiple performance technology projects within a performance improvement initiative • Develops plans for the coordination of multiple performance technology projects • Assembles and manages the necessary partners (internal and external to the organization) • Communicates among the partners to ensure success of the initiative • Responsible for the successful accomplishments of the performance improvement initiative
Advocate (internal and external partners)	• Communicates the benefits of the performance improvement initiative to internal and external partners • Works with partners to ensure alignment of strategic direction • Makes sure the initiative and related projects receive adequate support • Provides organizational "clout" to get performance interventions implemented • Serves as change agent within the organization
Steering Committee	• Provides direction and supervision to the design and development processes • Provides organizational "clout" to get performance interventions implemented • Members serve as change agents within the organization

(Continued)

Table 6.1 (continued)

Performance Intervention Project Manager	• Manages the design and development of specific performance technology interventions • Works with the initiative leader to ensure the alignment of performance technologies • Leads the technical development team • Is responsible for the accomplishments of specific performance technology interventions
Technical Development Team	• Provides the design and development support necessary for creating performance technologies that can accomplish desired results when implemented • Represents a range of professional backgrounds (e.g., information technology, human resources, instructional design, computer interfaces) necessary to support the design and development of distinct performance technologies • Creates draft products in the design and development of performance technology interventions • Obtains input and feedback on design and development products through formative evaluations • Revises design and development products as necessary
Non-Technical Development Staff Member	• Provides support and assistance in the design and development of performance technologies (often across multiple development projects) • Creates draft products in the design and development of performance technology interventions • Obtains input and feedback on design and development products through formative evaluations • Revises design and development products as necessary

(Continued)

Table 6.1 (concluded)

Production Coordinator	• Provides the expertise to produce materials (e.g., training manuals, job aids, user manuals) based on design documents • Facilitates the transition from development to implementation for performance technology projects
Subject Matter Expert	• Provides expert input into the design, development, and evaluation processes • Offers feedback on draft design and development projects

Case in Point

Landon and his team knew that they would have to focus on synergies and partnerships across the multiple interventions. Their improvement budget was small, so efficient processes were essential. Fortunately, the same experts and advocates would be useful for two or more solutions. By capitalizing on the work of one design project to inform the design of other related technologies, Landon was confident that they could succeed.

As an example, Regina from the manufacturing division agreed to be a project coordinator for the design and development of a new employee-retention program that will focus on the manufacturing, executive administrative, and human resources divisions. The team quickly realized that Regina should work closely with the new employee-orientation project team within human resources, as well as the workplace reengineering project team within the manufacturing division, as these were critical to the improvement initiative. Technical and non-technical team members were then assigned to all three of these closely aligned projects in order to make the most of limited resources.

Designing and Developing Solutions

It is now time for the design and development of each performance technology. Steps in the design and development of individual performance technologies are often specific and distinct, from the identification of ergonomic factors and the redesign of production lines to the sequencing of learning objectives and the selection of instructional techniques for training interventions. Luckily, there are many common steps that can be taken to successfully manage the design and development processes of most performance technologies.

A generic yet pragmatic design and development process focuses on results, bases decisions on systematic analysis, considers multiple options for each decision, and uses formative evaluations of interim products to improve results prior to implementation. Processes with these characteristics can be equally successful in guiding the design and development of electronic performance support systems, instructional events, career counseling programs, job aids, employee retention programs, knowledge management systems, and most any other performance technologies.

Step Three: Develop performance interventions.

Desired results: Performance technologies that are ready for implementation.

The specific design and development processes for performance technologies will vary, depending on the intervention's characteristics and specifications. For instance, to revise an existing rewards system, you will need a process quite different than the one you use to develop new multi-media training. While some interventions involve the development of new organizational policies, others require the development of storyboards or user interfaces. Therefore consider both the unique and universal aspects of each performance technology when planning its design and development.

A multi-purpose development process can, however, be used for numerous performance interventions. It isn't detailed enough to guide decisions for every aspect of your design and development process, yet it can guide you to the accomplishment of useful results. This generic process provides both basic guidelines and a structure for your improvement efforts.

The Basics of Design and Development

1. **Review performance objectives.** Review the performance objectives to define the precise results that are expected from the performance technology.

2. **Review performance assessments.** Review the performance assessments to verify how the results of the performance technology will be measured.

3. **Examine options for success.** Identify multiple techniques and tactics for effectively designing and developing the products. From internal project teams and outsourcing to management by objective and situational leadership, there are always options for how the design and development process will be conducted.

4. **Create a management plan.** Create a management plan that is based on the selected techniques and tactics. Be sure to include interim and final deliverables, milestone products that can measure your success along the way, due dates, names of individuals or teams with primary product responsibilities, contingency plans for known risks, development procedures, formative evaluation objectives, and communication and change-management tasks. All tasks should have defined products and deliverables that provide measurable results for monitoring performance.

5. **Obtain partner agreement and support.** Share the design and development management plan with the partners and team members to ensure that you have adequate support and resources for each task. It is also important to review the project timeline with team members to verify that it is achievable.

6. **Execute the plan.** Implement the project management plan to accomplish the identified milestone products and project deliverables.

7. **Review interim draft products.** The results of each task from the project plan should be reviewed to determine if they provide the necessary inputs (i.e., results) for the subsequent tasks and deliverables.

8. **Revise products as required.** Make necessary revisions based on feedback regarding the interim draft products that are produced during the design and development processes.

(Continued)

9. **Test deliverables.** When interim products lead to the development of a project deliverable (e.g., a new interview protocol to be used in recruiting, an online training program, or an improved communications system for workforce safety), conduct formative evaluations of the products.

10. **Revise deliverables as required.** Make necessary revisions based on feedback from the formative evaluations.

11. **Develop an implementation and evaluation plan.** Create detailed plans for the processes and actions you require. In this plan, you should include a timeline for evaluating the success of performance technology based on the criteria set out in the performance objectives.

12. **Produce final deliverables.** When formative evaluations of distinct deliverables have been conducted and the necessary revisions to the deliverables have been made, complete production of the final deliverables required for implementation.

Use this general process as a foundation; then tailor the steps and procedures to your set of specific technologies. For specific performance technologies (e.g., training, incentive systems, strategic planning, balanced scorecards, process redesign, position recruitment), you can customize the basic steps to focus on the identified performance requirements. Table 6.2 illustrates how the foundational steps of the general process can be integrated into the design processes of specific performance technologies.

Table 6.2. General design and development processes
for sample performance technologies

Electronic Performance Support System

1. Analyze performance requirements.
2. Complete a task and performance analysis.
3. Define system specifications.
4. Identify integrated performance assessments.
5. Select performance support requirements.
6. Define media and software requirements.
7. Create rapid prototype of support system and do formative evaluation.
8. Review and revise, based on formative evaluations.
9. Complete development of performance support system and do formative evaluation.
10. Review and revise as required.

Process Reengineering

1. Analyze performance requirements.
2. Complete a task analysis.
3. Complete a performance analysis.
4. Compare current and desired processes.
5. Identify redundancies and opportunities for improvement.
6. Brainstorm improvements with partners.
7. Define potential variations to related processes.
8. Review and revise proposed processes, based on expert input.
9. Prioritize and select new processes, based on performance requirements.
10. Develop training or support systems necessary for new process implementations.
11. Complete a pilot test of new processes.
12. Revise the processes, as required.

Balanced Scorecard[2]

1. Analyze performance requirements.
2. Identify critical success factors.
3. Identify and define appropriate performance measures for financial, external, internal, and innovation perspectives.
4. For each measure, collect baseline data.

(Continued)

Table 6.2 (continued)

5. For each measure, identify desired performance standards based on objectives at the societal, organizational, and individual/team levels.
6. Review and revise performance measures, as necessary.
7. Identify performance gaps or measures.
8. Define implications of performance gaps.
9. Create action plans for addressing performance gaps.
10. Monitor action plan implementations.
11. Review, revise, and repeat process, as necessary.

Classroom Instruction[3]

1. Analyze performance requirements.
2. Identify instructional goals.
3. Complete instructional analysis.
4. Define entry behaviors and learner characteristics.
5. Determine criterion-referenced test items.
6. Select instructional strategy.
7. Develop instructional materials.
8. Conduct formative evaluations.
9. Complete a summative evaluation based on performance requirements.

Systemic Strategic Planning[4]

1. Analyze performance requirements.
2. Identify collaboration partners.
3. Create a societal-level Ideal Vision.
4. Derive an organizational-level Mission Objective.
5. Define individual/team-level performance objectives.
6. Review and revise for alignment.
7. Conduct needs assessment.
8. Prioritize needs for closure.
9. Create a communication plan.
10. Review, revise, and repeat process, as necessary.

Mentoring Program

1. Analyze performance requirements.
2. Define desired results for protégés and mentors.
3. Complete task and performance analyses for mentoring processes.

(Continued)

Table 6.2 (concluded)

4. Identify measures for assessing results of mentoring processes. 5. Determine protégé–mentor matching process. 6. Develop necessary training or support systems necessary for mentoring processes. 7. Complete a pilot test of the mentoring program. 8. Review and revise the program, as required.

Aligning Project Accomplishments and Tasks

Remember that most improvement efforts call for several perform-ance technologies, each with its own design and development processes. You can nevertheless capitalize on the unique and shared steps you find among these processes. Make the most of the similarities, maximize the benefits of the unique aspects, and continually verify the alignment of all performance interventions included in your set of solutions.

It is important that you maintain a systemic perspective. Be sure to monitor the accomplishments and tasks of each develop-ment project to identify where processes can and should be improved. Look for similar resource requirements, update roles and responsibilities, and confirm that each process remains focused on the accomplishment of assigned performance objectives.

Step Four: Align the common and the unique.

Desired results: Documentation that all design and development processes have been reviewed for opportunities to improve efficiency and effectiveness.

Begin by making an inventory of tasks within each design and development process. Identify the milestones and deliverables (i.e., products), as well as the tactics and processes that will be utilized. It is often best to begin by listing project deliverables for each proc-ess (e.g., an analysis report on employee perspectives of a current manufacturing process; a software product to measure customer service response times; a just-in-time job aid for calculating cus-tomer orders). Each step in the design and development process should be linked to project deliverables and performance objectives. You can then list the tactics and processes associated with those products (e.g., needs assessment of manager performance, analysis of the workplace performance environment, focus groups with senior managers).

The results of each design and development process should contribute to the production of one or more performance technologies and the accomplishment of associated performance objectives. In turn, each performance technology should contribute to the achievement of one or more organizational objectives. The accomplishment of societal objectives is the result of contributions from multiple organizations. This important alignment is only possible when you maintain a systemic perspective.

Chapter Summary

The accomplishment of useful results is completely dependent on the design and development processes. Earlier planning steps are essential for success, but without the actual development (and later implementation) of performance interventions, there would be no results. Identify the tasks, roles, responsibilities, milestones, timelines, and performance requirements for each performance technology before beginning any design and development steps. Review each process, and the entire set of solutions, for opportunities to improve efficiency.

Each performance technology (e.g., balanced scorecard, employee recruiting, work station redesign, inventory tracking software) will require its own design and development process. The characteristics and unique requirements of each can guide the steps used to accomplish its performance objectives. Customize a general design and development process to define specific project tasks and milestones.

Continue to focus on achieving useful results. The results of each design and development process should align performance at the individual/team (micro), organizational (macro), and societal (mega) levels.

Chapter 6 Notes

1. Lick and Kaufman, 2000

2. See Kaplan and Norton, 1993

3. Based on Dick, Cary, and Carey, 2001

4. Based on Kaufman, Watkins, and Leigh, 2001

Section Three:
Continual Improvement

Do not expect results at every level right away. Many individual or team results must be accomplished before organizations can achieve their performance objectives. Societal results rely on the contributions of many organizations. As a consequence, performance is often improved only incrementally.

The challenge is to set incremental milestones that offer the opportunity to demonstrate meaningful results without driving the activities to either the pace of the tortoise or the hare. Defining incremental improvements that are minor will lead to performance technology projects that never end. Likewise, those that are too significant can place a performance improvement initiative on a path toward failure. You must find balance and periodically reaffirm that all processes remain aligned with the achievement of desired results.

Every initiative to improve performance should include a formative evaluation cycle during the development phase and a long-term plan for continual improvements during implementation. Improving the results and processes during both improvement cycles will be described in these next two chapters.

Figure 7.0. The Performance by Design framework

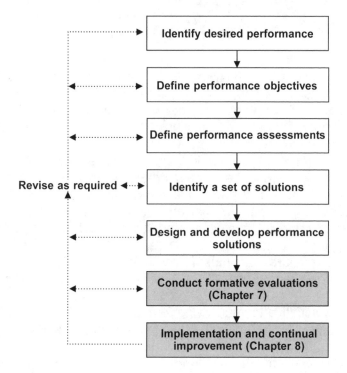

Chapter 7
Conduct Formative Evaluations

Introduction

Formative evaluations allow users, experts, small groups, and others to take a good look at deliverables prior to implementation. More than just interim revisions or updates, formative evaluations are formal processes with specific design and development considerations (see Figure 7.1). During formative evaluation, you can pilot test performance technologies in the performance environment, share early products with expert performers, and/or reassess your development processes. In all cases, formative evaluations will provide you with essential feedback that can shape later results.

Figure 7.1. Process for completing formative evaluations

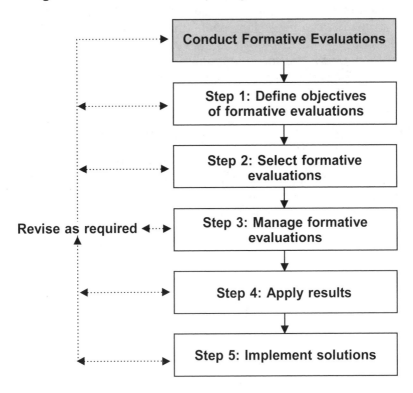

Formative evaluations facilitate the development of effective interventions. They link design and development efforts to the requirements of successful implementation. The key tasks of formative evaluations are:

- Assess performance.
- Receive feedback.
- Document recommendations and changes.

You must have input into the revision process and make it part of the development life cycle. From specific information (such as which process steps are not sequenced accurately or which software operations are not functioning) to general concerns (such as employee attitudes about a policy change), feedback should guide the revision of all project deliverables.

Documenting recommendations that are based on formative evaluations is especially important when you have multiple performance technology projects that are closely related and that share performance objectives. Document the evaluation processes, the feedback received, and the subsequent revisions to each performance technology; the lessons-learned during formative evaluations of one project can help improve the results of other design and development efforts as well.

Lastly, continually assess each technology's potential to accomplish desired results. Reviews of draft materials (e.g., products, reports, analysis results, design documents) can be used to verify the alignment of interim results with associated performance objectives. Formative evaluations should also include pilot testing of pre-release performance interventions to assess their effectiveness in the performance environment.

The Performance by Design approach includes two closely related, yet distinct, formative evaluation processes. The first evaluations take place within the design and development efforts of each performance technology, focusing on improving the accomplishments of the performance technology. (Make them part of all systematic design and development processes.) The second evaluations assess the overall performance improvement initiative, including each of the coordinated performance technologies selected to achieve results at the societal, organizational, and individual/team levels. This second set of evaluations does not focus solely on the improvements of any specific performance technology, but rather on the system of performance technologies being created collaboratively (often associated with organizational and societal results). The evaluation processes, tasks, and steps described in this chapter can and should be applied to evaluations with either focus: technology-specific or initiative-wide. Together, the formative evaluations with each focus provide the systemic feedback necessary to accomplish consistent, long-term, and useful results.

Case in Point

The collaborative teams throughout Pill Containers used the next few weeks to develop the selected performance technology interventions. As the projects progressed, the improvement team planned and carried out formative evaluations. They collected feedback, documented input, and assessed the performance of several interventions. This effort to conduct essential evaluations at the same time was completed before any technologies were actually implemented.

The improvement team routinely selected which formative evaluations would take place, and which formative evaluation methods would be used. They worked with the project coordinators to identify appropriate questions, materials, techniques, and protocols for obtaining valuable information that could be used for improving design and development processes and accomplishments. By working with each of the performance technology projects, the improvement team was able to maintain consistency, perform adequate formative evaluations, preserve a results-focus, and document all of the valuable information that was provided by the participants in the formative evaluations. In addition, the improvement team shared lessons learned with each project across the organization.

Evaluations with Results

All performance improvement processes, including formative evaluations, should be results-driven. From interim improvements (which typically lead to second and third drafts of materials, policies, or reports) to pilot tests of complete performance interventions, formative evaluations are designed to accomplish valuable results. Hence, you begin the formative evaluation process by defining the performance objectives that will be accomplished (i.e., the results and expectations of each selected evaluation process).

Don't select or plan any formative evaluation steps (e.g., focus groups, pilot tests, expert interviews) until you have identified the desired results and assessed your options based on what accomplishments they can achieve. The performance data that results from a formative evaluation can then be used to make improvements prior to implementation. Focus each evaluation on either single performance solutions or previously defined clusters.

Step One: Define objectives for formative evaluations.

Desired results: Detailed list of priority achievements that must be accomplished by selected formative evaluation processes.

Start by defining the results to be accomplished by the formative evaluations. Given the variations among the performance objectives associated with each performance technology being developed, specify evaluation objectives for each development project independently (or in previously defined clusters). You can often capitalize on similar evaluation objectives among performance technologies associated with similar performance objectives.

Here are some sample objectives for formative evaluations of individual performance technologies:

- The formative evaluation will produce a content review of a newly developed training seminar on project management.

- The formative evaluation will assess the percentage of performers who can demonstrate accurate use of a performance checklist.

- The formative evaluation will document supervisors' ability to enter necessary data into the new performance management software program.

- The formative evaluation will assess employee attitudes with regard to the new incentive policies for quality controls at satellite company locations.

In addition, also identify evaluation objectives for the broader performance improvement efforts. Here are several objectives for the improvement of a multi-faceted performance initiative:

- The formative evaluation will document the accomplishment of all internal performance objectives.

- The formative evaluation will assess customer attitudes regarding new processes implemented through perform-ance improvement efforts.

- The formative evaluation will examine the collaborative accomplishment of two or more associated performance technologies.

- The formative evaluation will verify that the performance technologies do not violate organizational policies or legal requirements.

- The formative evaluation will assess the impact of perform-ance improvement efforts on second- and third-generation clients.

Your formative evaluation processes should be guided by the required results. Systematically identify and implement appropriate evaluation tools and techniques, listing the guiding objectives for each formative evaluation before planning any evaluation activities. Be sure to use precise objectives that state the expected results. You can again use the SMARTER framework to verify the com-pleteness of your objectives (refer back to Table 3.2).

Evaluation Techniques

Formative evaluations can be conducted in numerous ways, using a variety of techniques and a range of participant groups. A variety of data-collection techniques are commonly used to assess the quality and effectiveness of the performance technology prior to imple-mentation (e.g., individual interviews, focus groups, pilot tests, document reviews). Accordingly, each evaluation technique has strengths and weaknesses that should be considered in determin-ing which will best accomplish your objectives. Commonly, forma-tive evaluation processes include multiple formative evaluation techniques. This integration of multiple techniques can help you collect the valuable information you will use to make improvements prior to implementation.

Identify several evaluation techniques for each objective and then review the multiple techniques to see which ones work best. Each technique can be evaluated on its capacity to accomplish the performance objectives within the constraints of the project or initia-tive. Use the formative evaluation objectives (along with contextual issues like time requirements, financial resources, available participants, etc.) to prioritize and select data-collection techniques. (It can be helpful to identify any measures that you will use to judge the success of each formative evaluation to guide prioritization and selection).

Step Two: Select formative evaluations.

Desired results: A list of the formative evaluation processes selected for each evaluation objective.

You should select a combination of evaluation techniques that will provide adequate and useful information for making improvement decisions. Focus your selection on the results (i.e., objectives) defined for each formative evaluation. The data collected during the formative evaluations will then help you improve the separate performance technologies, and/or the results to be accomplished by the overarching improvement efforts prior to implementation.

Many data-collection techniques can be employed in formative evaluations. Highlighted below are several of the most common techniques for collecting valuable information.

One-on-one reviews. One-on-one reviews focus on the performance technology products (e.g., organizational policies, training materials, software applications, job aids), as well as any design documents (e.g., story boards, results from prototypes, performance objectives) that are the results of the design and development efforts. Participants in the process typically review each product in detail with the designer, developer, and/or project manager. Participants should be encouraged to discuss the strengths and weaknesses of individual products with the project representative, as well as recommended changes, alternative approaches, and suggest tactics for a successful implementation. The one-on-one review should be conducted in a relaxed setting where participants can openly discuss the opportunities for improving the results that will be achieved by the performance technology.

One-on-one reviews should not be an individual pilot test or trial run of the performance technology. Instead, the reviews should focus on the detailed discussions of each applicable product from the design and development effort (e.g., design documents, sample user interfaces, storyboards, draft policies). Include at least one expert performer in the one-on-one reviews as part of the formative evaluation process. Additional reviews with novice and/or intermediate performers can also supplement the process with valuable information.

Performance Observations. Performance observations can be a valuable way to determine if particular aspects of the performance intervention achieve the desired results. By utilizing discrete products of the performance technology interventions, individual or group performance observations can identify opportunities for improving the results. Provide the participants with the relevant products from the design and development process, and observe the application of those products in the performance environment. A performance observation differs from a field trial (or pilot test) in that representative designers, developers, and/or managers interact with participants during the process to ask questions, provide clarification, and assess the distinct elements within the performance technology.

For example, performance observations during the development of a new employee recruitment process might include evaluating participants by using an online recruiting tool, testing new competency indicators, practicing new interview techniques, or trying out several new performance simulations. Each of the tested products can then be improved before being combined into a single performance technology for implementation.

Discuss with the participant the pros and cons of using the performance technology and go over their recommendations for improving the results (e.g., the system for matching new employees with mentors doesn't consider non-work interests). Record and analyze the results of each performance observation and then document any improvements made to the performance technology. When performance observations are not feasible, consider using performance "diaries" (or logs) for the individual application of performance technology products.

Focus Group Reviews. Small-group reviews can provide valuable information regarding the effectiveness of the specific performance technology or general improvement efforts. Focus group reviews are not pilot tests or trial runs of the performance technology. Rather, they provide the opportunity for multiple participants (with varied interests, expertise, and experience) to review and discuss the performance technology products. Typically, focus groups are provided with significant products from the development efforts (e.g., nearly complete drafts of organizational policies, training materials, software applications, job aids) and asked to complete a structured review process. After each individual participant has had the opportunity to review the provided products, the facilitator of the focus group leads a planned discussion focused on the anticipated results of implementing the performance technology, the opportunities for improving the performance of the technology, and so on.

Large-group surveys. Surveys are a valuable technique for collecting data on attitudes and past experiences. As a process for accumulating soft data that is not independently verifiable, surveys are most appropriate for measuring the important perceptions that a number of employees, clients, or other organizational partners have regarding the performance technology or broader improvement efforts. Since the implementation of new performance technologies generally requires change within the organization, data regarding the perceptions of individuals representing multiple perspectives is often of great value.

You can often identify opportunities for improvement prior to implementation by collecting data from a variety of perspectives. Since surveys rarely include the opportunity for participants to complete a trial application of the performance technology, most often you will collect data regarding anticipated use and perceptions of anticipated value. Review and analyze aggregated data as well as data from each perspective separately. Then look for opportunities to improve the performance solutions and their upcoming implementation.

Performance data. Collect performance data for the discrete components of a performance technology. Useful information for making improvements prior to implementation is often found in performance data, so don't wait for the complete performance before collecting it. For instance, in designing and developing a new Web-based training management system, collect performance data on individual elements of the system as they are developed (e.g., the interface to load new users into the system, the database that manages course enrollments) to ensure that each attains the desired results. Only when all subsystems with the performance technology have been formatively evaluated should you pilot test the complete performance technology in the performance environment.

Pilot test. The pilot test (or field trial) mirrors the intended application of the performance technology in the performance environment as closely as possible. In the pilot test, include multiple participants who represent the relevant user groups. To the extent possible, give participants in the pilot test the opportunity to use the performance technology in an environment that is reflective of their work setting (without input from designer, developer, or others conducting the formative evaluation). Data from performance logs, performance observations, post-performance participant comments, and/or performance diaries can all be used to provide feedback from the pilot test.

A systematic formative evaluation identifies opportunities to make beneficial improvements. Use more than one data-collection technique in most formative evaluations. Multiple iterations of each technique can then be used to improve the reliability of resulting data. When selecting evaluation techniques, you should align each with the associated evaluation objectives. You can then select techniques based on their relative strengths and weaknesses (see Table 7.1).

Table 7.1. Advantages and Disadvantages of
Formative Evaluation Techniques[1]

Data-Collection Tool or Technique	Types of Data Available	Advantages	Disadvantages
One-on-one Reviews	Soft qualitative	• Allows for follow-up questions • Can show commitment • Permits a detailed review • Offers a comfortable environment for feedback	• Is time- and resource-intensive • Doesn't provide for anonymity • Lone interviewee might not have necessary expertise
Performance Observation (single source)	Soft qualitative	• Provides data about actual performance • Allows for perceptions of performance to be included in data	• Restricted to observation periods • Not independently verifiable
Performance Observation (multiple sources)	Hard quantitative	• Provides data about actual performance • Allows for perceptions of performance to be included in data	• Restricted to observation periods
Focus Group (group interview)	Soft qualitative	• Allows for follow-up questions • Can show commitment • Group members can expand on the ideas of others • No single individual has to have comprehensive expertise	• Is somewhat time- and resource-intensive • Doesn't provide for anonymity • Not all participants will be able to give feedback • "Group-think" can occur

(Continued)

Table 7.1 (concluded)

Large-group Survey (Likert-type scale questionnaire)	Soft quantitative	• Requires less time from respondents • Is quantifiable for descriptive statistics	• Takes time to develop and validate • Restricted to questions on survey • Often confused as hard data
Large-group Survey (opinion questionnaire)	Soft qualitative	• Requires less time of respondents • Offers open-ended questions for longer and more-detailed responses	• Requires time-consuming qualitative analysis • Number of questions might have to be limited • Restricted to questions on survey
Performance Data	Hard quantitative	• Provides data about actual performance • Allows for performance comparisons in individuals or groups • Doesn't require additional time	• Limited to data collected • Might not reveal reasons for performance gaps • Limited to "what is"
Pilot Test (field trial)	Hard/Soft qualitative	• Complete technology can be tested within the performance environment • Provides performance data from all components of the intervention to the evaluation process	• Can be time- and resource-intensive • Must have characteristics of the performance environment

Evaluation Management

Managed processes are more likely to accomplish desired results. That's why you will want to plan, implement, and revise your formative evaluation processes, just as you would do for other aspects of performance improvement. From identifying the necessary resources to describing how participants will be recruited, evaluations are important in the development of effective performance technologies, and hence warrant thorough planning and management.

Step Three: Manage formative evaluations.

Desired results: A management plan that coordinates the results, processes, roles, responsibilities, timelines, milestones, and other implementation aspects of the formative evaluations.

Planning for formative evaluations must be done early in the design and development process. The right time to begin evaluation planning is when you have first selected the performance technologies. Consider results, techniques, and sequencing to ensure that you have adequate time and resources available for making necessary revisions.

Include in your evaluation management plan information regarding which target groups can provide useful information, which individuals will collect and analyze data, and how improvement decisions will be made. Decide the number of participants you want for each evaluation technique, steps for recruiting appropriate participants, the number of evaluation repetitions required to verify data reliability, and the expected products that will result from the evaluation effort. Much like any other project plan, evaluation planning should cover performance objectives, milestones, tasks, individual roles, and other items that define how the formative evaluations will be conducted and what you want to accomplish.

Specify in the plan how the specific data-collection techniques will be implemented, and how progress will be measured. The evaluation process will require participation and input from individuals and groups that are not necessarily working on the development project. The steps taken to recruit, motivate, and engage participants should also be monitored to ensure adequate participation.

After the formative evaluations are complete, systematically communicate the results to the appropriate individuals, teams, and partners. Likewise, ask for feedback on how to improve future evaluations. The findings from this reflective exercise can then be used for other ongoing design and development projects.

Improving Performance

Formative evaluations help verify whether or not you are likely to achieve the results you want. (This is valuable information prior to implementation of any performance technology.) Therefore, as part of your performance improvement effort, develop a systematic process for documenting recommendations, making revisions, and reevaluating the resulting products. Use this process to make the constructive improvements to each and every performance solution. Remember that in addition to making improvements to specific performance technologies, you are also using formative evaluations to improve the results across collaborative improvement efforts. Use data collected for each individual performance technology to determine how improvements can be made elsewhere within the project.

Recommendations from formative evaluations can also be useful in making improvements during implementation. For example, cross-functional training might not be within the current budget of a performance technology project, although it is an improvement worth making. Save the recommendation, and perhaps it will become a feasible option after the initial implementation has produced baseline results.

Step Four: Apply evaluation results.

Desired results: Improved results from each performance technology.

The first task in applying the results of formative evaluations is to inventory and compare the findings from each of the separate evaluation techniques. This process gives you the opportunity to assess and analyze the feedback from the multiple participants and perspectives. In the analysis, look for similarities, contradictions, recommendations, and opportunities to capitalize on related performance improvement activities.

When we teach a teenager to drive a car, we balance the technical details (e.g., shifting gears, using the clutch, monitoring speed, using the mirrors) and the bigger-picture requirements that are necessary for successful driving (e.g., safety, responsibility, accountability). Similarly, when using formative evaluations to improve performance, balance the recommendations for specific revisions to a performance technology with those related to the bigger-picture accomplishments. Continually relate all improvement to the achievement of societal, organizational, and individual/team results. It is often tempting to focus too closely on the operational details of a single performance technology (e.g., more video elements in an e-learning course, or policy changes for improving the work environment), but you will risk losing sight of the long-term organizational objectives that are to be achieved (e.g., zero safety-related defects, zero workplace accidents) and their related societal outcomes (e.g., zero disabilities from accidents). In response, apply the results of the formative evaluations to improvements at all levels of the Organizational Elements Model (i.e., Inputs, Processes, Micro results, Macro results, and Mega results).[2]

Prioritize the recommendations based on the potential value (e.g., effectiveness, efficiencies) they add to performance and the potential costs (in time, money, resources) associated with their implementation. Not all recommendations will lead to change right away. Some recommendations will have to be cataloged for use in subsequent improvement efforts, while others will be applied in related improvement projects. All reasonable recommendations should, however, be documented and prioritized.

Monitor the status of each recommendation selected for the revision process. Minor revisions to a performance technology typically only require that you document the completed revision, but broader or more complex revisions may warrant another series of formative evaluations to ensure that the revisions are giving you the results you want. If you apply a systematic approach to making revisions, you can then document and justify the improvement to be made.

Be sure to inform all evaluation participants of the resulting revisions that were made based on their feedback. Communicating the results of their input is an important step in gaining support for implementation (as well as for future design and development efforts).

Case in Point

The improvement team at Pill Containers used performance observations to formatively evaluate several products involved in the development of the new knowledge management system. In each case, the team watched as individual employees tried to answer practical questions using the new database. From problems with the user interface to technical glitches when certain key words were used in the search, information from the formative evaluations helped improve the system prior to implementation.

(Continued)

Case in Point (continued)

A variety of formative evaluation techniques had to be used because of the diversity of improvement projects already being done within the organization. Each development project used formative evaluation techniques that were based on their specific information requirements for making improvements. All projects did, however, complete a pilot test in the performance environment prior to implementation.

The results from each formative evaluation session were communicated back to the related design and development projects. In addition, the performance improvement team turned many of the recommendations into "best practices" that were shared among the project coordinators of the various development projects within the initiative. This helped those working on other efforts avoid many of the obstacles and problems faced by their colleagues.

As it documented the feedback, the improvement team recorded important information on a spreadsheet: The name of the individual or group that provided the feedback, the date of the feedback, the date that the feedback was communicated to the appropriate project coordinators, and the status of how the feedback was addressed in the revisions (when applicable). The team closely monitored progress and communicated effectively with participants about how their input was used.

Implement Interventions

Results do not get accomplished without action. At some point, you have to implement your performance technologies to achieve your performance objectives. Implementation can be as short as a one-hour motivation workshop or as long as an initiative that becomes part of your standard operating procedures, or simply consist of the introduction of a new job aid. The benefits of systematic planning, assessing, developing, and evaluating should be evident in the results. Implementations, however, are most effective when they are organized, structured, and managed.

Up to this point in the design and development of performance technologies, there have been relatively few changes to the processes and procedures used within the organization to achieve results. During implementation, the performance improvement initiative will begin to change how things are done within the organization, as well as what results are measured. Changes in each of these can strain employees and organizational partners as they strive to perform within this new environment. Managing the implementation process and the ensuing changes within the organization is essential.

Step Five: Implement solutions.

Desired results: Accomplishment of the performance objectives at the societal, organizational, and individual/team levels.

Performance improvement initiatives are never perfect when they are initially implemented. While formative evaluations can vastly improve the efficiency and effectiveness of technology interventions prior to implementation, there are always additional opportunities to make useful improvements. The transition from formative evaluations to implementation can therefore be awkward if you haven't planned for its success. There is no formula for calculating the ideal time for this transition, but when you find that formative evaluations are only producing recommendations that have little impact on the achievement of performance objectives, you can be confident that it's time to begin implementation.

There are two general tasks related to implementing performance technology solutions: managing processes, and monitoring results. From scheduling meetings to ensuring that resources are available when required, try to actively manage the many processes that are related to successful implementation. Assist in planning for the implementation of each performance solution. Maintain a focus on achieving results at all levels. Guide implementation teams in making critical decisions. Direct the communication with internal and external partners. Work to ensure that the changes in the organizational environment do not overwhelm those responsible for applying the improvement efforts.

Measuring the achievement of performance objectives and determining if adequate contributions are being made are just two of the implementation steps that can benefit from active monitoring of performance. You should routinely measure your success to verify that necessary results are being accomplished at the societal, organizational, and individual/team levels.

Chapter Summary

Formative evaluations provide valuable information for making improvements prior to implementation. Each evaluation has established objectives that can guide decisions. In addition, a combination of evaluation techniques should be used to produce valuable information for making improvement decisions. Systematic improvements can then be identified for each performance technology as well as for the overall improvement effort.

While there are always opportunities to make further improvements to performance interventions, organizations cannot wait for perfection when desired results are not being accomplished. Transitioning from formative evaluation to implementation is an essential part of achieving of useful results. The timing of this transition from development to implementation will typically vary from project to project, but you have to implement it if you want results. Continue, however, to make systematic improvements to each performance solution throughout implementation.

Chapter 7 Notes

1.   Kaufman, Watkins, and Leigh, 2001

2.   Kaufman, 1992; 1998

Chapter 8
Continual Improvements

Introduction

Every stage in a performance improvement effort is an opportunity to gather and use new information. Continuous improvement, in fact, should be an ongoing goal and part of every organization's culture. From small tweaks that can improve process efficiencies to broader performance reviews to ensure that performance solutions are working, use the continual improvement process to achieve desired results.

At the time of implementation, no performance solutions will be picture perfect; there will always be opportunities to improve processes, procedures, techniques, tools, resources, and implementation tactics. Acknowledge these normal shortcomings by providing a systematic process by which current applications of performance technologies can be improved upon (see Figure 8.1).

Figure 8.1: Continual improvement process

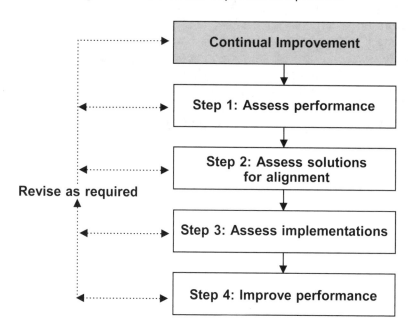

Measuring Results

Not all performance solutions will contribute useful results, at least not at first. Improvements will routinely have to be made to most performance efforts in order for desired results at all levels to be accomplished. Regularly assess and monitor the results being accomplished, and then verify that those results are aligned with desired performance objectives at the societal, organizational, and individual/team levels. Measure current accomplishments against the desired results defined in each performance objective to identify new opportunities for improvement.

Use the same performance assessments you used to judge potential performance solutions. Since all decisions regarding the initial design and development of each performance technology were based on the achievement of these results, it is only reasonable to use them as standards for performance during implementation.

An organization's strategic direction can also shift in the middle of an improvement effort. If it does, performance objectives that were drivers for early decisions may have to be adjusted. Review (and possibly revise) the related performance objectives for each performance technology. Based on your review, decide if the selected performance technologies can accomplish the newly identified results, if current interventions can be revised, or if an alternative set of solutions should be considered.

When is it time to start over? Significant changes in the strategic objectives of your organization (or its partners) suggest that you should again select, design, and develop appropriate performance technologies.

Step One: Assess performance.

Desired results: An analysis report of the results being accomplished by implemented performance solutions.

Performance should be measured systematically and routinely. Implementation is not the time to identify results to be achieved or how those accomplishments will be measured. Regularly revisit the performance assessments and apply those measures to evaluate your success.

Use the assessments aligned with societal and organizational performance objectives to evaluate the accomplishments of the systemic performance improvement effort. Individual and team-level assessments can then be used to measure the performance of specific technologies.

During the planning stage (i.e., determining the performance objectives that will guide decisions), you used performance objectives sequentially from each level to define desired results (only later identifying desired processes and inputs). Correspondingly, when evaluating (i.e., assessing the achievement of results), you should reverse the sequence. First evaluate at the Input level, and then the process, micro, macro, and mega levels in that order.

As you move sequentially from society to organization to individual during the planning stages and from individual to organization to society during the implementation and evaluation stages, you will achieve the strategic goals and objectives of the organizational partners (see Figure 8.2).

Figure 8.2. Relating the levels of the Organizational Elements Model in planning, implementing, and evaluating[1]

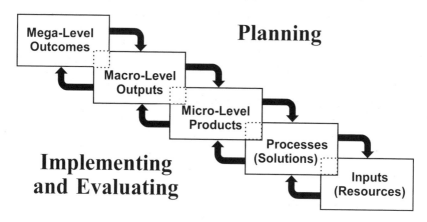

When you identify performance solutions that aren't accomplishing desired results (or that are inefficient), review their selection, design, development, and implementation for opportunities to improve. You may find that the selected performance technology was not the right choice, or you overlooked things during the design process or made errors during implementation. It is important, however, that you evaluate each performance technology using only the performance measures agreed upon at the beginning of the design process. If those measures (or associated objectives) have changed, then the entire improvement process should be reviewed and possibly revised.

Review Solutions for Alignment

When you find discrepancies between current and desired results (i.e., needs), first see if there are any conflicts or redundancies leading to these less than desirable accomplishments. A review of performance technologies and their associated performance objectives will help you to identify any misalignments that have developed during your development and implementation processes.

Step Two: Assess solutions for alignment.

Desired results: A document describing (or illustrating) the current alignment of performance solutions and desired results.

Begin by reviewing your performance objectives, performance analysis, and selected performance technologies. You should especially examine the relationships between implemented performance technologies and their associated performance objectives. Also look for contributing factors that were not addressed during the implementation or suboptimization resulting from opposing efforts among selected solutions.

Sometimes a breakdown in the alignment will be obvious. During implementation, for example, you might realize that a new performance appraisal program is indeed assisting individuals in developing realistic performance expectations, but a new rewards or incentive program is still supporting older performance objectives. The alignment between the two programs is thus an issue you would want to examine and possibly address.

At other times, it will take more investigating to identify why desired results are not being accomplished. Examine the records from each step in the selection, design, and development process to identify possible failures, misunderstanding, or miscommunication. Look specifically for processes that didn't lead to desired results. Also, use this review to revisit the earlier decisions from a new perspective. Work closely with internal and external partners, since they may be better able to spot opportunities to improve.

Implementation Effectiveness and Efficiency

The third step in making continual improvements is to review the implementation of each performance technology. Several might not be producing the anticipated or desired results. Unanticipated problems during the design and development are likely reasons why a performance technology may fail to achieve the desired results. Even the best implementation effort rarely goes as planned, so also look for unexpected challenges encountered during implementation. Review each product, process, procedure, and task associated with each technology to determine if there are opportunities to improve the results being achieved.

Step Three: Assess implementations.

Desired results: A comprehensive review of the achievements from each technology implementation.

Review the implementation of each performance technology for both effectiveness and efficiency. Did the implantation achieve each of the interim results that were necessary for its success? Did the implementation efficiently use resources and build on the experiences of other improvement efforts? The answers to these questions will often lead you to opportunities for improvement.

Let's say, for example, that a communications Web site is part of your performance improvement initiative. If it is not accomplishing its desired results, then you should look not only at the selection, design, and development documents, but also at the implementation process. Elements within the Web site may have been dropped during implementation. Perhaps there were technical problems that delayed the inclusion of essential functions. Review the intended and actual implementation processes for each performance technology carefully, since this is often where good solutions go off course.

As you perform each review, take time to focus on the current resource requirements (e.g., time, money, personnel) to identify opportunities to improve efficiency (i.e., achieve the desired results with less demand on the individuals and/or organization). Improving the efficiency of each performance technology is important if you want to sustain long-term improvements.

Case in Point

When all of the pilot tests had been done and final revisions had been made, Pill Containers began implementation of eight perform-ance technologies. The improvement team monitored the results of each intervention using the same performance assessments identi-fied during the planning phases of the improvement initiative. Several performance technologies achieved many of the desired results upon initial implementation, but the team decided to monitor the progress of all performance technologies for several months in order to collect longitudinal data.

Using the performance assessments, data were collected and analyzed regularly by the improvement team to identify trends and opportunities to coordinate implementations. Landon and the team reserved judgment on the effectiveness of technology projects that did not initially accomplish the desired results until after adequate data was collected. The performance improvement team met again several weeks later to review the results of the eight interventions implemented by this time (with the remainder still completing their formative evaluation cycles). Only three failed to produce the results that had been the focus of design and development.

The results from the balanced scorecard program, for instance, were limited. Given the improvements outlined at the last perform-ance review, the team recommended that a follow-up round of formal evaluations be completed to determine if additional "tweaks" to the program could be made. In addition, the team identified several dis-crepancies between the mentoring program that was designed and the mentoring program that had actually been implemented. The team responded by recommending that a new implementation plan be developed with more-specific guidelines.

Unfortunately, a process reengineering effort that was designed and developed in the accounting division also produced limited results. The improvement team concluded that mistakes were made in per-formance analysis that probably led to an inappropriate solution for the given performance objectives. Instead of providing additional resources for making improvements to the program, the team recom-mended that a second performance analysis be completed.

Making Improvements

Improvements to performance require action. From misalignments between solutions and objectives to implementations that meet unanticipated resistance, opportunities to improve have to be acted on if useful results are going to be achieved. Revise each performance solution whenever there is evidence that you can better accomplish desired results. Use a combination of hard and soft data to verify opportunities to improve in specific areas.

Step Four: Improve performance.

Desired results: Accomplishment of the performance objectives at every level.

Regularly review the results of every performance technology, assessing performance against the agreed-upon objectives. During these reviews, look for opportunities to improve alignment of interventions, the effectiveness of specific technologies, and/or the efficiency of solutions. Keep a list of the various improvement opportunities associated with each performance objective and develop a prioritized schedule for making changes. Prioritize improvements based on associated benefits and costs in time, resources, and people.

For each of the selected improvements, create a detailed implementation plan. Some improvements may only require the addition of a feedback element in an electronic performance support tool, while others may require revisions to complex organizational policies. The scope of an improvement plan varies; your plan should make the necessary revisions without creating $1,000 solutions to $5 problems.

As with most implementation efforts, follow your improvement implementation plan and monitor results regularly to make sure the changes are useful. Don't assume that all improvements will immediately lead to desired results. As we said earlier, performance improvements are normally incremental. Continue to make improvements to the performance system, even if you do not initially accomplish your performance objectives, until you achieve desired results.

Case in Point

It had been over a year since Landon had first met with the members of the performance improvement team. This was a good time for him to reflect on the year's accomplishments. The approach and processes they had used at Pill Containers illustrated how a systematic process for selecting, designing, and developing effective performance technologies can be applied within most any organization. Many of the selected performance technologies are now helping the company achieve valuable performance objectives, a fact that he never forgot to mention to his supervisor.

From working closely with internal and external partners to evaluating the success of each performance technology, these were just a few of the practical steps the team took to improve performance. The challenges and opportunities they found along the way were nevertheless characteristic of most any improvement efforts. Now Landon hoped that he could share these experiences with other professionals at an upcoming conference.

Landon was especially proud of the team's never-ending commitment to the achievement of results. He knew that because of that relentless focus on performance, this project was much more successful than if they had simply given division managers the training they asked for.

Even after they implemented initial performance solutions, the team continued to take a systematic, results-focused approach to improving performance. Improving upon their earlier improvement efforts turned out to be the key to finally accomplishing performance objectives at the individual/team, organizational, and societal levels. All the team members recognized that success rarely comes overnight; they knew it was critical that they regularly assess how well each performance technology was meeting their long-term goals and objectives. When new performance objectives were identified (or when old objectives were updated with new criteria or assessments), they returned to the design process and repeated many of the steps again.

On the whole, it had been a very successful year. The improvement efforts were considered a success by almost all of the internal and external partners. A meeting was scheduled to gain review the

(Continued)

Case in Point (continued)

agreed upon performance objectives with the few remaining skeptics. The systematic selection, design, and development of useful performance technologies had paid off for everyone: Landon, the improvement team, the Pill Containers organization and its external partners, and even their shared society.

Chapter Summary

Unanticipated design flaws and implementation problems are common during the launch of any new program or project. For that reason, you must retain realistic expectations of what performance technologies can achieve when they are first introduced and implemented. In addition, you should develop a systematic process for making continual improvements to each and every performance technology throughout their implementation. Include in your process a review of the current alignment between implemented solutions and performance objectives, the performance contributions of individual technology interventions, and the opportunities to make implementation processes more efficient.

Continue to measure the success of each performance solution, based on the agreed-to performance objectives that guided their initial selection, design, and development. Use data from the performance assessments to further refine and improve on the results already being accomplished. The continual improvement of performance technologies is a recurring process that you should guide, manage, and monitor throughout the entire performance improvement effort. Even when desired results are being achieved, you can use the continual improvement process to look for new opportunities or ways to improve the efficiency of current processes.

Chapter 8 Note

1.   See Kaufman, Oakley-Brown, Watkins, and Leigh, 2003

Conclusion

The desire to achieve useful results should guide your decisions on a daily basis. From routine choices to extraordinary judgments, the successful achievement of valuable results (i.e., performance) should be closely tied to the strategic ambitions of our organizations and communities. Goals that are meaningful to the partnership of our organizations and society are the guides that each of us should use in our professional practice. Working together, we can achieve worthy results, improve lives, help communities, meet financial targets, and improve performance.

The success and merits of a performance improvement effort is directly related to the results it achieves and the contributions it makes to the organization, its partners, and society. For this reason, the Performance by Design approach aligns all decisions about what should be done with agreed-upon objectives of what should be accomplished. The steps, processes, procedures, techniques, and tools in the Performance by Design framework then help guide you through the selection, design, and development of performance technologies that achieve useful results. Each step along the way is focused on contributing to your success as well as the success of others.

Every performance improvement initiative should use multiple performance technologies that are aligned with the performance objectives of the organization and its partners. Postpone the selection of any specific performance technologies (including organizational favorites such as training, strategic planning retreats, and executive coaching) until after the results to be accomplished have been defined and their measures agreed upon. Even when organizational leaders begin an improvement effort with desired solutions already in mind, defining desired results before identifying useful processes is a necessary prerequisite for success.

Achieving results that are *useful* is only possible when you use a systemic and systematic process to evaluate options. For this reason, you should identify multiple options for accomplishing your performance objectives. Each of these can then be assessed and evaluated as part of the systematic selection process.

Once a set of capable solutions has been selected, you can then design and develop interventions that will achieve useful results. Each unique design and development project will include tasks such as analyzing performance gaps, selecting a design team, formally evaluating performance technology solutions, and continually improving performance during implementation. While Performance by Design provides a general framework for this, you should be prepared to customize it for each performance technology.

After your performance interventions are designed and developed, you can use a variety of formative evaluation techniques to improve their quality prior to implementation. Listen to focus groups, experienced performers, and others as they provide you with useful recommendations for improving selected performance technologies before they are implemented. Their guidance is priceless.

Throughout implementation, continually review and revise each performance technology. Maintain your focus on the accomplishment of useful results and let your performance objectives guide your improvement decisions. By aligning all that your organization uses, does, produces, and delivers with the contribution of useful results to external clients and societal partners, you can ensure the long-term success of any performance improvement efforts. While other processes offer quick-fixes and paths toward implementing "favorite" solutions, useful performance improvements begin and end with a focus on societal contributions.

Always begin with a clear and measurable definition of what results you want to accomplish. This can (and should) guide all of your decisions along a path toward the achievement of useful results.

Glossary of Terms[1]

This glossary includes definitions already provided. This is a complete summary of important terms and concepts.

System, systems, systematic, and systemic: related but not the same

system approach: Begins with the sum total of parts working independently and together to achieve a useful set of results at the societal level, adding value for all internal and external partners. We best think of it as the large whole and we can show it thus:

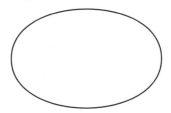

systems approach: Begins with the parts of a system—subsystems—that make up the "system." We can show it thus:

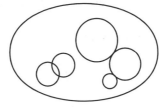

It should be noted here that the "system" is made up of smaller elements, or subsystems, shown as bubbles embedded in the larger system. If we start at this smaller level, we will start with a part and not the whole. So, when someone says they are using a "systems approach" they are really focusing on one or more subsystems, but they are unfortunately focusing on the parts and not the whole. When planning and doing at this level, they can only assume that the payoffs and consequences will add up to something useful to society and external clients, and this is usually a very big assumption.

systematic approach: An approach that does things in an orderly, predictable, and controlled manner. It is a reproducible process. Doing things, however, in a systematic manner does not ensure the achievement of useful results.

systemic approach: An approach that affects everything in the system. The definition of *the system* is usually left up to the practitioner and may or may not include external clients and society. It does not necessarily mean that when something is systemic it is also useful.

Now, let's turn to other strategic thinking and planning terms.

AADDIE model: The ADDIE model with the vital function of Assessment added to the front of it.

ADDIE model: A contraction of the conventional instructional systems steps of Analysis, Design, Development, Implementation, and Evaluation. It ignores or assumes a front determination through assessment of what to analyze, and it also assumes that the evaluation data will be used for continuous improvement.

change creation: The definition and justification, proactively, of new and justified as well as justifiable destinations. If this is done before change management, acceptance is more likely. This is a proactive orientation for change and differs from the more usual *change management* in that it identifies in advance where individuals and organizations are headed rather than waiting for change to occur and be managed.

change management: Ensuring that whatever change is selected will be accepted and implemented successfully by people in the organization. Change management is reactive in that it waits until change requirements are either defined or imposed and then moves to have the change accepted and used.

comfort zones: The psychological areas, in business or in life, where one feels secure and safe (regardless of the reality of that feeling). Change is usually painful for most people. When faced with change, many people will find reasons (usually not rational) for why not to make and modifications. This gives rise to Tom Peter's (1997) observation that "it is easier to kill an organization than it is to change it."

constraints: Anything that will not allow one to meet the results specifications. These might arise from many sources, including not enough resources, insufficient time, political pressures, and the like.

costs-consequences analysis: The process of estimating a return-on-investment analysis before an intervention is implemented. It asks two basic questions simultaneously: what do you expect to give and what do you expect to get back in terms of results? Most formulations do not compute costs and consequences for society and external client (Mega) return on investment. Thus, even the calculations for standard approaches steer away from the vital consideration of self-sufficiency, health, and well-being (Kaufman.1998, 2000).

criteria: Precise and rigorous specifications that allow one to prove what has been or has to be accomplished. Many processes in place today do not use rigorous indicators for expected performance. If criteria are "loose" or unclear, there is no realistic basis for evaluation and continuous improvement. Loose criteria often meet the comfort test, but don't allow for the humanistic approach to care enough about others to define, with stakeholders, where you are headed and how to tell when you have or have not arrived.

deep change: Change that extends from Mega—societal value added—downward into the organization to define and shape Macro, Micro, Processes, and Inputs. It is termed *deep change* to note that it is not superficial or just cosmetic, or even a splintered quick fix. Most planning models do not include Mega results in the change process, and thus miss the opportunity to find out what impact their contributions and results have on external clients and society. The other approaches might be termed *superficial change* or *limited change* in that they only focus on an organization or a small part of an organization.

desired results: Ends (or results) identified through needs assessments that are derived from soft data relating to "perceived needs." *Desired* indicates these are perceptual and personal in nature.

ends: Results, achievements, consequences, payoffs, and/or impacts. The more precise the results, the more likely that reasonable methods and means can be considered, implemented, and evaluated. Without rigor for results statements, confusion can take the place of successful performance.

evaluation: Compares current status (what is) with intended status (what was intended) and is most commonly done only after an intervention is implemented. Unfortunately, *evaluation* is used for blaming and not fixing or improving. When blame follows evaluation, people tend to avoid the means and criteria for evaluation or leave them so loose that any result can be explained away.

external needs assessment: Determining and prioritizing gaps, then selecting problems to be resolved at the Mega level. This level of needs assessment is most often missing from conventional approaches. Without the data from it, one cannot be assured that there will be strategic alignment from internal results to external value added.

hard data: Performance data that are based on objectives and independently verifiable. This type of data is critical. It should be used along with "soft" or perception data.

Ideal Vision: The measurable definition of the kind of world we, together with others, commit to help deliver for tomorrow's child. An Ideal Vision defines the Mega level of planning. It allows an organization and all of its partners to define where they are headed and how to tell when they are getting there or getting closer. It provides the rationality and reasons for an organizational mission objective.

Inputs: The ingredients, raw materials, and physical and human resources that an organization can use in its processes in order to deliver useful ends. These ingredients and resources are often the only considerations made during planning without determining the value they add internally and externally to the organization.

internal needs assessment: Determining and prioritizing gaps, then selecting problems to be resolved at the Micro and Macro levels. Most needs assessment processes are of this variety (Watkins, Leigh, Platt, & Kaufman, 1998).

learning: The demonstrated acquisition of a skill, knowledge, attitude, and/or ability.

learning organization: An organization that sets measurable performance standards and constantly compares its results and their consequences with what is required. Learning organizations use performance data, related to an Ideal Vision and the primary mission objective, to decide what to change and what to continue—it learns from its performance and contributions. Learning organizations may obtain the highest level of success by strategic thinking: focusing everything that is used, done, produced, and delivered on Mega results—societal value added. Many conventional definitions do not link the "learning" to societal value added. If there is no external societal linking, then it could well guide one away from the new requirements.

Macro level of planning: Planning focused on the organization itself as the primary client and beneficiary of what is planned and delivered. This is the conventional starting and stopping place for existing planning approaches.

means: Processes, activities, resources, methods, or techniques used to deliver a result. Means are only useful to the extent that they deliver useful results at all three levels of planned results: Mega, Macro, and Micro.

Mega level of planning: Planning focused on external clients, including customers/citizens and the community and society that the organization serves. This is the usual missing planning level in most formulations. It is the only one that will focus on societal value added: survival, self-sufficiency, and quality of life of all partners. It is suggested that this type of planning is imperative for getting and proving useful results. It is this level that Rummler refers to as *primary processes* and Brethower calls the *receiving system.*

Mega thinking: Thinking about every situation, problem, or opportunity in terms of what you use, do, produce, and deliver as having to add value to external clients and society. Same as *strategic thinking.*

methods-means analysis: Identifies possible tactics and tools for meeting the needs identified in a *system analysis.* The methods-means analysis identifies the possible ways and means to meet the needs and achieve the detailed objectives that are identified in this Mega plan, but does not select them. Interestingly, this is a comfortable place where some operational planning starts. Thus, it either assumes or ignores the requirement to measurably add value within and outside the organization.

Micro-level planning: Planning focused on individuals or small groups (such as desired and required competencies of associates or supplier competencies). Planning for building-block results. This also is a comfortable place where some operational planning starts. Starting here usually assumes or ignores the requirement to measurably add value to the entire organization as well as to outside the organization.

mission analysis: Analysis step that identified: (1) what results and consequences are to be achieved; (2) what criteria (in interval and/or ratio scale terms) will be used to determine success; and (3) what are the building-block results and the order of their completion (functions) required to move from the current results to the desired state of affairs. Most mission objectives have not been formally linked to Mega results and consequences, and thus strategic alignment with "where the clients are" are usually missing (Kaufman, Stith, Triner, & Watkins,1998).

mission objective: An exact, performance-based statement of an organization's overall intended results that it can and should deliver to external clients and society. A mission objective is measurable on an interval or ratio scale, so it states not only "where we are headed" but also adds "how we will know when we have arrived." A mission objective is best linked to Mega levels of planning and the Ideal Vision to ensure societal value added.

mission statement: An organization's Macro-level "general purpose." A mission statement is only measurable on a nominal or ordinal scale of measurement and only states "where we are headed" and leaves rigorous criteria for determining how one measures successful accomplishment.

need: The gap between current results and desired or required results. This is where a lot of planning goes "off the rails." By defining any gap as a *need,* one fails to distinguish between means and ends and thus confuses what and how. If *need* is defined as a gap in results, then there is a triple bonus: (1) it states the objectives (What Should Be), (2) it contains the evaluation and continuous improvement criteria (What Should Be), and (3) it provides the basis for justifying any proposal by using both ends of a need—What Is and What Should Be in terms of results. Proof can be given for the costs to meet the need as well as the costs to ignore the need.

needs analysis: Taking the determined gaps between adjacent organizational elements, and finding the causes of the inability for delivering required results. A needs analysis also identifies possible ways and means to close the gaps in results— needs—but does not select them. Unfortunately, *needs analysis* is usually interchangeable with *needs assessment.* They are not the same. How does one "analyze" something (such as a need) before they know what should be analyzed? First assess the needs, then analyze them.

needs assessment: A formal process that identifies and documents gaps between current and desired and/or required results, arranges them in order of priority on basis of the cost to meet the need as compared to the cost of ignoring it, and selects problems to be resolved. By starting with a needs assessment, justifiable performance data and the gaps between What Is and What Should Be will provide the realistic and rational reason for both what to change as well as what to continue.

objectives: Precise statement of purpose, or destination of where we are headed and how we will be able to tell when we have arrived. The four parts to an objective are (1) what result is to be demonstrated, (2) who or what will demonstrate the results, (3) where will the result be observed, (4) what interval or ratio scale criteria will be used? Loose or process-oriented objectives will confuse everyone (see Mager, 1997). A Mega-level result is best stated as an objective.

outcomes: Results and payoffs at the external client and societal level. Outcomes are results that add value to society, community, and external clients of the organization. These are results at the Mega level of planning.

outputs: The results and payoffs that an organization can or does deliver outside of itself to external clients and society. These are results at the Macro level of planning where the primary client and beneficiary is the organization itself. It does not formally link to outcomes and societal well-being unless it is derived from outcomes and the Ideal (Mega) Vision.

paradigm: The framework and ground rules individuals use to filter reality and understand the world around them (Barker, 1992). It is vital that people have common paradigms that guide them. That is one of the functions of the Mega level of planning and outcomes so that everyone is headed to a common destination and may uniquely contribute to that journey.

performance: A result or consequence of any intervention or activity, including individual, team, or organization: an end.

performance accomplishment system (PAS): Any of a variety of interventions (such as "instructional systems design and development," quality management/continuous improvement, benchmarking, reengineering, and the like) that are results oriented and are intended to get positive results. These are usually focused at the Micro/Products level. This is my preferred alternative to the rather sterile term *performance technology* that often steers people toward hardware and premature solutions (Kaufman,1999, 2000).

Processes: The means, processes, activities, procedures, interventions, programs, and initiatives an organization can or does use in order to deliver useful ends. While most planners start here, it is dangerous not to derive the Processes and Inputs from what an organization must deliver and the payoffs for external clients.

products: The building-block results and payoffs of individuals and small groups that form the basis of what an organization produces and delivers, inside as well as outside of itself, and the payoffs for external clients and society. Products are results at the Micro level of planning.

quasi-need: A gap in a method, resource, or process. Many so-called "need assessments" are really quasi-needs assessments since they tend to pay immediate attention to means (such as training) before defining and justifying the ends and consequences (Watkins, Leigh, Platt, & Kaufman, 1998).

required results: Ends identified through needs assessment, which are derived from hard data relating to objective performance measures.

restraints: Possible limitations on what one might use, do, and deliver. Restraints serve as a type of performance specification.

results: Ends, products, outputs, outcomes—accomplishments and consequences. Usually misses the outputs and outcomes.

soft data: Personal perceptions of results. Soft data is not independently verifiable. While people's perceptions are reality for them, they are not to be relied on without relating to "hard"—independently verifiable—data as well.

strategic alignment: The linking of Mega-, Macro-, and Micro-level planning and results with each other and with Processes and Inputs. By formally deriving what the organization uses, does, produces, and delivers to Mega/external payoffs, strategic alignment is complete.

strategic thinking: Approaching any problem, program, project, activity, or effort by noting that everything that is used, done, produced, and delivered must add value for external clients and society. Strategic thinking starts with Mega.

tactical planning: Finding out what is available to get from What Is to What Should Be at the organizational/Macro level. Tactics are best identified after the overall mission has been selected based on its linkages and contributions to external client and societal (Ideal Vision) results and consequences.

wants: Preferred methods and means assumed to be capable of meeting needs.

What Is: Current operational results and consequences. These could be for an individual, an organization, and/or for society.

What Should Be: Desired or required operational results and consequences. These could be for an individual, an organization,
and/or society.

wishes: Desires concerning means and ends. It is important not to
confuse *wishes* with *needs.*

Making Sense of Definitions and Their Contribution to a Mega Perspective

Here are some ground rules for strategic thinking and planning:

1. System Approach ≠ Systems Approach ≠ Systematic Approach ≠ Systemic Approach

2. Mega-level Planning ≠ Macro-Level Planning ≠ Micro-Level Planning

3. System Analysis ≠ Systems Analysis

4. Means ≠ Ends

5. Hope ≠ Reality

6. Outcome ≠ Output ≠ Product ≠ Process ≠ Input

7. There are three levels of planning: Mega, Macro, and Micro, and three related types of results: Outcomes, Outputs, Products.

8. Need is a gap in results, not a gap in Process or Input.

9. Needs Assessment ≠ Needs Analysis (nor front-end analysis or problem analysis)

10. Strategic Planning ≠ Tactical Planning ≠ Operational Planning

11. Change Creation ≠ Change Management

Glossary of Terms Notes

[1] Based on Kaufman, R., & Watkins, R. (2000, April). Getting serious about results and payoffs: We are what we say, do, and deliver. *Performance Improvement, 39* (4), 23–31.

References

Barker, J. A. (1992). *Future Edge: Discovering the New Paradigms of Success.* New York: William Morrow and Co., Inc.

Barker, J. A. (2001). *The New Business of Paradigms.* St. Paul, Minnesota: Star Thrower Distribution. Videocassette.

Brethower, D. M. (2005, February). Yes we can: A rejoinder to Don Winiecki's rejoinder about saving the world with HPT. *Performance Improvement, 44*(2), 19–24.

Brethower, D. M. and P. C. Dams. (1999: Jan.). Systems thinking (and systems doing). *Performance Improvement,* 38 (1), 37–52.

Capon, C., and A. Disbury. *Understanding Organizational Contexts.* England: Financial Times/Prentice Hall.

Clark, R. E., and F. Estes. (2002). *Turning Research into Results: A Guide to Selecting the Right Performance Solutions.* Atlanta, Georgia: CEP Press.

Dick, W. L., and J. Cary. (2001). *The Systematic Design of Instruction.* New York: Longman.

Gerson, R. (2006). The missing link in HPT. *Performance Improvement.* Vol. 45, No. 1, 10-17.

Gilbert, T., and M. Gilbert. (1989: Jan.) Performance engineering: Making human productivity a science. *Performance and Instruction.* Vol. 28, No. 1, 3–9.

Gilbert, T. (1978) *Human Competence: Engineering Worthy Performance.* New York: McGraw-Hill.

Graham, S., J. F. Wedman, T. Tanner, and C. Monahan (1998). Yes, classroom sales training can enhance performance. *Performance Improvement Quarterly,* Vol. *11*(2), 101–112.

Harless, J. H. (1975). *An Ounce of Analysis is Worth a Pound of Objectives.* Newnan, Georgia: Harless Performance Guild.

Kaplan, R., and P. Norton (1993). Putting the balanced scorecard to work. *Harvard Business Review* (September/October, 134–147).

Kaufman, R. (2006). *Change, Choices, and Consequences: A Guide to Mega Thinking.* Amherst, Massachusetts: HRD Press.

Kaufman, R. (1992). *Strategic Planning Plus.* Thousand Oaks, California: Sage Publishing.

Kaufman, R. (1998). *Strategic Thinking: A Guide to Identifying and Solving Problems.* Washington, D.C. and Arlington, Virginia: The International Society for Performance Improvement and the American Society for Training and Development.

Kaufman, R. (2000). *Mega Planning: Practical Tools for Organizational Success.* Thousand Oaks, California: Sage Publications.

Kaufman, R., H. Oakley-Brown, R. Watkins, and D. Leigh. (2003). *Strategic Planning for Success: Aligning People, Performance, and Payoffs.* San Francisco, California: Jossey-Bass.

Kaufman, R., M. Stith, D. Triner, and R. Watkins. (1998). The changing corporate mind: Organizations, vision, mission, purposes, and indicators on the move toward societal payoffs. *Performance Improvement Quarterly, 11*(3), 32–34.

Kaufman, R., and R. Watkins. (1996). Cost-consequences analysis. *Human Resources Development Quarterly, 7*(1), 87–100.

Kaufman, R., and R. Watkins. (1999). Needs assessment. In Langdon, D. (ed.), *The Resource Guide to Performance Interventions.* San Francisco, California: Jossey-Bass.

Kaufman, R., and R. Watkins. (2000). Getting serious about results and payoffs: We are what we say, do, and deliver. *Performance Improvement Journal, 39*(4), 23–32.

Kaufman, R., R. Watkins, and D. Leigh. (2001). *Useful Educational Results: Defining, Prioritizing, and Achieving.* Lancaster, Pennsylvania: Proactive Publishing.

Kaufman, R., R. Watkins, and L. Sims. (1997). Cost-consequences analysis: A case study. *Performance Improvement Quarterly, 10*(2), 7–21.

Kirkpatrick, D. (1959). *Evaluating Training Programs* (2nd ed.). San Francisco, California: Berrett Koehler.

Leigh, D. (2006). SWOT analysis. In Pershing, J. (ed.), *The Handbook of Human Performance Technology.* San Francisco, California: Jossey-Bass/Pfeiffer.

Leigh, D. (2003). Worthy Performance, Redux. PerformanceXpress. International Society for Performance Improvement newsletter. (Available online: http://www.performancexpress.org/0306)

Leigh, D., R. Watkins, W. Platt, and R. Kaufman. (2000). Alternate models of needs assessment: Selecting the right one for your organization. *Human Resource Development Quarterly, 11*(1), 87–93.

Lick, D., and R. Kaufman. (2000). Change Creation: The rest of the planning story. In *Technology-Driven Planning: Principles to Practice.* J. Boettcher, M. Doyle, and R. Jensen (eds.). Ann Arbor, Michigan: Society for College and University Planning.

Mager, B., and R. Pipe. (1997). *Analyzing Performance Problems.* (3rd ed.). Atlanta, Georgia: The Center for Effective Performance.

Peters, T. (1997). *The Circle of Innovation: You Can't Shrink Your Way to Greatness.* New York: Knopf.

Robinson, D. G., and J. C. Robinson. (1995). *Performance Consulting: Moving Beyond Training.* San Francisco, California: Berrett Koehler.

Rossett, A. (1987). *Training Needs Assessment.* Englewood Cliffs, New Jersey: Educational Technology Publishing Co.

Rossett, A. (1999). *First Things Fast.* San Francisco, California: Jossey-Bass.

Scriven, M. (1967). The methodology of evaluation. In Tyler, R. W., Gagne, R. M., and Scriven, M. (eds.). *Perspectives of Curriculum Evaluation.* Chicago, Illinois: Rand McNally.

Stolovitch, H. (2000). Research and theory to practice. In *Performance Improvement, 39*(4), 7–16.

Stolovitch, H. (2002). Front-end analysis, implementation planning, and evaluation: Breaking out of the Pamela syndrome. *Performance Improvement, 41*(4), 5–7.

Watkins, R. (2006). Aligning Performance Technologies with Organizational Strategic Plans. In Pershing, J. (ed.), *The Handbook of Human Performance Technology*. San Francisco:Jossey-Bass/Pfeiffer.

Watkins, R., and J. Wedman. (2003). A process for aligning performance improvement resources and strategies. *Performance Improvement Journal, 42*(7), 9–17.

Watkins, R., and R. Kaufman. (2002). Assessing and evaluating: Differentiating perspectives. *Performance Improvement Journal, 41*(2), 22–28.

Watkins, R., and D. Leigh. (2001). Performance improvement: More than bettering the here and now. *Performance Improvement Journal, 40*(8), 10–15.

Watkins, R., R. Kaufman, and D. Leigh. (2000). A scientific dialogue: A performance accomplishment code of professional conduct. *Performance Improvement Journal, 39*(4), 17–22.

Watkins, R., and R. Kaufman. (1999). Strategic planning. In Langdon, D. (ed.), *The resource guide to performance interventions.* San Francisco, California: Jossey-Bass.

Watkins, R., D. Leigh, W. Platt, and R. Kaufman. (1998). Needs assessment: A digest, review, and comparison of needs assessment literature. *Performance Improvement Journal, 37*(7), 40–53.

Watkins, R., D. Leigh, R. Foshay, and R. Kaufman. (1998). Kirkpatrick plus: Evaluation and continuous improvement with a community focus. *Educational Technology Research and Development Journal, 46*(4).

Wedman, J. F., and L. L. Diggs. (2001). Identifying barriers to technology-enhanced learning environments in teacher education. *Computers in Human Behavior, 17*(4), 421–430.

Wedman, J. F., and S. W. Graham. (1998). Introducing the concept of performance support using the performance pyramid. *Journal of Continuing Higher Education, 46*(3), 8–20.

Witkin, B. R., and J. W. Altschuld. (1995). *Planning and Conducting Needs Assessments: A Practical Guide.* Thousand Oaks, California: Sage Publications.

About this Series

Defining and Delivering Successful Professional Practice—HPT in Action

This is the third of six books to define and deliver measurable performance improvement. Each volume defines a unique part of a fabric: a fabric to define, develop, implement, and continually improve human and organizational performance success. In addition, the series relates to the professional standards in the field.[1]

Why This Series?

Human and Organizational Performance Accomplishment—some call the field HPT (Human Performance Improvement)—is of great interest to practitioners and clients alike who intend to deliver successful results and payoffs that are based on research, ethics, and solid concepts and tools. The author of each book provides a practical focus on a unique area, and each book is based on 10 principles of professional contribution.

Each book "stands alone" as well as knits with all the others. Together they:

1. Define the field of HPT and performance improvement based on the principles of ethical and competent practice.

2. Provide specific guidance on six major areas of professional practice.

3. Are based on a common framework for individual and organizational performance accomplishment.

4. Reinforce the principles that drive competent and ethical performance improvement.

There is a demand for an integrated approach to Human and Organizational Performance Accomplishment/Human Performance Technology. Many excellent books and articles are available (some by the proposed authors), but none covers the entire spectrum of the basic concepts and tools, nor do they give the integrated alignment or guidance that each of these six linked books provides.

This series is edited by Roger Kaufman (Ph.D., CPT), Dale Brethower (Ph.D.), and Richard Gerson (Ph.D., CPT).

The six books and the authors are:

Book One: *Change, Choices, and Consequences: A Guide to Mega Thinking and Planning.* Roger Kaufman, Professor Emeritus, Florida State University, Roger Kaufman & Associates, and Distinguished Research Professor, Sonora Institute of Technology

Book Two: *Defining What to Do and Why.* Dale Brethower, Professor Emeritus, Western Michigan University and Research Professor, Sonora Institute of Technology

Book Three: *Performance by Design.* Ryan Watkins, Associate Professor, George Washington University, Senior Research Associate, Roger Kaufman & Associates, and former NSF Fellow

Book Four: *Achieving High Performance.* Richard Gerson, Ph.D., CPT, Gerson Goodson, Inc.

Book Five: *Implementation and Management of Solutions.* Robert Carlton, Senior Partner, Vector Group

Book Six: *Evaluating Impact: Evaluation and Continual Improvement for Performance Improvement Practitioners.* Ingrid Guerra-López, Ph.D., Assistant Professor, Wayne State University and Associate Research Professor, Sonora Institute of Technology as well as Research Associate, Roger Kaufman & Associates

How This Series Relates to the Professional Performance Improvement Standards

The following table identifies how each book relates to the 10 Standards of Performance Technology[2] [identified by numbers in parentheses ( ) pioneered by the International Society for Performance Improvement (ISPI).[3] In the table on the following page, an "X" identifies coverage and linking, and "✓" indicates major focus].

This series, by design, goes beyond these standards by linking everything an organization uses, does, produces, and delivers to adding measurable value to external clients and society. This six pack, then, builds on and then goes beyond the current useful criteria and standards in the profession and adds the next dimensions of practical, appropriate, as well as ethical tools, methods, and guidance of what is really required to add value to all of our clients as well as to our shared society.

	Focus on Results	Take a System Approach	Add Value	Partner	Needs Assessment	Performance Analysis	Design to Specification	Selection, Design, & Development	Implementation	Evaluation & Continuous Improvement
	(1)	(2)	(3)	(4)	(5)	(6)	(7)	(8)	(9)	(10)
Book 1	✓	✓	X	✓	✓	X	X	X		✓
Book 2	X	✓	✓	X		✓	✓			X
Book 3	X	X	X			✓	✓	✓		X
Book 4	X	X	X	X		✓	X	✓	✓	X
Book 5	X	✓	✓	✓		✓	✓		✓	✓
Book 6	✓	✓	✓	X	✓				X	✓

All of this will only be useful to the extent to which this innovative practice becomes standard practice. We invite you to the adventure.

Roger Kaufman, Ph.D., CPT
Dale Brethower, Ph.D.
Richard Gerson, Ph.D., CPT

Endnotes

1. The Standards of Performance Technology developed by the International Society for Performance Improvement, Silver Spring, Maryland.

2. Slightly modified.

3. Another approach to standardization of performance are a set of competencies developed by the American Society for Training and Development (ASTD), *ASTD Models for Human Performance Improvement,* 1996, which are more related to on-the-job performance.

About the Author

Ryan Watkins is an associate professor of educational technology at George Washington University in Washington, D.C. He received his doctoral degree from Florida State University in instructional systems design, and has additional formal training in performance improvement, Web design, change management, and program evaluation. Ryan designs and teaches courses in instructional design, distance education, needs assessment, system analysis and design, research methods, and technology management for online and classroom delivery. He has been a visiting scientist with the National Science Foundation, a professor of instructional technology and distance education at Nova Southeastern University, and a member of the research faculty in the Learning Systems Institute's Center for Needs Assessment and Planning at Florida State University.

He has written several books, including *75 E-Learning Activities: Making Online Courses More Interactive* (Jossey-Bass, 2005) and *E-Learning Companion: A Student's Guide to Online Success* (Houghton Mifflin, 2005). He co-authored *Strategic Planning for Success: Aligning People, Performance, and Payoffs* (Pfeiffer, 2003), and *Useful Educational Results* (ProActive: 2001). He has written more than sixty articles and book chapters on the topics of strategic planning, distance education, needs assessment, return-on-investment analysis, and evaluation. He served as vice president of the Inter-American Distance Education Consortium, and is an active member of the International Society for Performance Improvement and the United States Distance Learning Association.

Ryan offers a variety of workshops and consulting services on topics such as instructional design, performance improvement, interactive E-learning, and preparing learners for online success. He can be contacted at rwatkins@gwu.edu or www.ryanrwatkins.com.